Praise for *You Can't Stop the Growth*

"Chad Peterman offers a very unique perspective. As a very successful small business owner and a successful second-generation business owner he is in a very elite group of people. His wisdom on how to create a culture in the business that honors employees, customers, and generations of family members is truly unique. There are good business owners and then there are really good business owners who have grown a business and navigated succession from one generation to the next. This book is a treasure of leadership and business jewels that every small business owner should read."

—Jack Tester
President and CEO, Nexstar Network

"As a leader, getting the most out of the people around you is important when asking them to perform seemingly impossible tasks. Chad Peterman's ability to quickly connect with his team is nothing short of remarkable. He has proven to be a progressive, modern, and empathetic leader that is willing to take risks for the greater good of those he works for. His instinct to constantly empower those around him will prove to be valuable as Peterman continues to break barriers and scale without limits."

—Michael Crafton
President and CEO, Nelbud Service Group

"There is something here for everyone! If a rising tide raises all ships then Pete, Chad, Tyler, and all the great people at Peterman Heating, Cooling & Plumbing are that tide. An absolute must-read!"

—Mike Grimme

President, Johnstone Supply, Grimme Group

"Chad Peterman's new book, *You Can't Stop the Growth*, is an outstanding example of a leader who is determined and a true learner of the success principles of business and life. I met Chad when he joined my entrepreneurial business coaching program called Peak Performers, and as I grew to know him I was sincerely impressed with his unwavering commitment to learning.

"It is rare to meet someone this young with such a passion for wanting to improve his leadership skills to be the best in today's world. As I read this book I see that Chad has a true visionary ability to not only grow his company but also grow his employees to be true leaders, therefore not only helping their own families but also attracting the best customers possible. I would highly recommend this book to anyone who wants to improve yourself and others in the service world.

"This book is a heartwarming testimonial of a man who loves his family, his business, and being of service to his customers. We need more Chad Petermans in the world!"

—Lee Milteer

Business and Life Strategist
Best-selling author of Success Is an Inside Job

"The Peterman Company is one of Indianapolis's great success stories. Organically grown to become one of the city's largest heating, cooling, and plumbing companies, Peterman has been true to its roots of service, culture, and leadership. Beginning with Pete Peterman's family-oriented mentality for service, his sons have embraced his values and are well positioned to launch the business into the next generation. My company values culture above all other aspects of the business after profitability. There is no question in my mind the culture of Peterman Heating, Cooling & Plumbing will continue to firmly plant them as the hallmark of the HVAC and plumbing service business in Indiana and beyond. This book gives a great look into an even better business."

—Ryan Hasbrook

Co-founder and Chief Executive Officer, Eight Eleven Group

"I have known the founder, Pete, for many years, and this book is a tribute to how one man's vision can become reality through hard work, care, and compassion. This book describes the culture put in place by Pete and carried on by Chad and Tyler that looks to serve employees who ultimately take care of each customer. Inspiration can be found throughout if you are looking to build a powerful culture in your business or looking for evidence of a company intent on serving a larger purpose."

—Frank Kolisek, MD

Hip and Knee Surgeon, OrthoIndy

"In a world full of organizations racing toward gains at all costs and sometimes human expense, Peterman Heating, Cooling & Plumbing has built an enduring and beloved business that dedicates itself to growing and caring for its own people above all else. Chad Peterman candidly explains what's necessary to create a strong culture that acts as a magnet for attracting like-minded people dedicated to humbly serving others with gratitude. A great read for those interested in building a growth organization the right way, not the easy way."

—Jonathan Bancroft

President and CEO, Morris-Jenkins

Author of Mr. Jenkins Told Me ...: Forgotten Principles That Will Grow Any Business

"In his book *You Can't Stop the Growth*, Chad highlights the concept of what makes businesses run—people. He shares his unique and compelling strategies on how to grow. It's a must-read for anyone trying to create an enduring, great company."

—Jamie Gerdsen

President and CEO, Apollo Home

"Chad's passion for his employees shines through and his sincere focus on investing first in his people is a great reminder that it's not only the right thing to do, but it can unlock transformational business success. There is also something very powerful when leaders truly connect with and empower their front-line team."

—Jeff Wells, MD

President and Co-founder, OurHealth

"Pete, Chad, and Tyler Peterman have set the gold standard on growing a business by first growing people. In our world, where so many are struggling to find purpose, the Petermans' love for their team and their customers is playing out in a beautiful way—where purpose is clear, service is full-circle, growth is creating opportunity, and lives are being changed. This is the story of a great family working to reach their full potential but with the full intention of making sure every one of their employees also reaches their full potential. They have energized me to redouble my efforts to do the same with my team."

—Brett D. Bean

Founder and CEO, FE Moran Security Solutions

"I've witnessed Chad's commitment to excellence and to serving others, starting when we played on the same defense for Wabash College. Chad consistently was the first one in the film room and last one out of the weight room. His work ethic, character, and compassion are now on display and making a huge impact on the employees and customers of Peterman HVAC and Plumbing. I've recently had personal experience with Peterman team members and I was impressed with the knowledge, professionalism, and kindness of the customer service folks as well as the service provider. People truly do matter to Chad and his team and it is on display both internally and externally. Lastly, I love that Chad is bringing functional benefits and unique experiences to the company, and frankly the entire HVAC and plumbing industry, that actually positively impact his employees and add value to their lives. These benefits and experiences include but are not limited to continuing education and self-enrichment opportunities, birthday holidays, being present in interviews and reviews as an owner, and facilitating opportunities for employees to personally get to know each other. I'm excited to see Peterman Heating, Cooling & Plumbing grow, evolve, and continue to positively impact people's lives through providing quality services to customers and through creating even more engaging, value-added, and meaningful employment experiences."

—Frank Knez

Friend and Founder, K1ds Count, LLC

"People are our most important resource. We can always buy more equipment or bid more jobs, but if we don't develop our people, we can't proceed any further. In this book, Chad demonstrates the power that can be generated by investing in your people and allowing them to grow. If you are looking for a resource to help you develop a culture where your people can thrive, then look no further."

—Casey Dillon

CEO, Atlas Excavating, Inc.

"Peterman Heating, Cooling & Plumbing built a strong company culture based on its dedication to their employee's success. Pete Peterman created this foundation and this vision continues with Chad and Tyler. In *You Can't Stop the Growth*, Chad shares his successful strategies of leading, motivating, and empowering employees resulting in impressive growth and success. This is a must-read for everyone who realizes that people are the most important resource in their organization."

—Brian Habegger

President and CEO, The Habegger Corporation

"Chad Peterman's discussion of business culture surpasses simple motivational phrases. His unique business culture is a way of life for Peterman and his team. Having had the opportunity to interact with his team several times a year, I am continually impressed with his company operations. On every level, from ownership on, motivation to serve is paramount with a professional attitude and a sense of humor. The jovial manner with which Peterman and his team achieve their goals is refreshing and contagious. This successful growth model greatly benefits his customer base as well as each member of his stellar team. Chad Peterman's approach is a proven method to grow your business and retain a high-quality team."

—Thad David

Master Trainer, Nexstar Network

"The success of Peterman Heating, Cooling & Plumbing is a clear testament that building a culture rooted in caring for your team members and empowering them to succeed will lead to success. The Peterman family has done an incredible job of honoring the legacy and roots of their company while also adapting for the future and successfully transitioning to the next generation of family leadership."

—Daniel Maddox

CEO, Citizens State Bank

"Chad Peterman is a servant leader and mature beyond his years. His autobiographical book thoughtfully captures and concretely expresses timeless truths about leadership. He ascribes appropriate credit to his father's guiding worldview and influences, but Chad's adaptations and applications are his own. 'The Peterman way'—the 'employee [and their family]-first' perspective—focuses on professional and personal well-being and produces a positive, productive, and profitable workplace (and a fulfilling home life). His deliberate focus on identifying and grooming the next generation of leaders from within is far too rare in any industry. As a four-year Peterman customer, I can attest without reservation to the extraordinary emphasis on establishing and maintaining high-trust relationships built on quality service and world-class workmanship. I am a lifelong student of servant and situational leadership and Chad Peterman has produced a worthy addition to my library. Well done, sir. HOO-AAH!"

—Brian R. Copes
Brigadier General, Army (Retired)
President and Chief Executive Officer, Helping Veterans and Families (HVAF of Indiana, Inc.)

"It's truly an honor to work with the Peterman team. Chad and Tyler are a true representation of what Dad and Mom raised, two outstanding young men. The Petermans have a humble pursuit for business excellence while delivering a great work environment. Peterman is the type of company you would want to work in your home. As Peterman's business coach for Nexstar it has been such a joy to see Chad and the team take the industry's best practices and implement with their own management team. The Peterman team has managed their growth and massaged their culture at the same time to create a truly dynamic company. Can't wait to see what the future holds for the Petermans."

—John Conway
Nexstar Business Coach, Nexstar Network

"I completely agree with the Peterman philosophy that leadership starts within. I personally believe that values are the foundation that habits are built upon. In this book, Chad Peterman illustrates that all great organizations start with a core belief system and the corresponding practices that reinforce the culture. By understanding and challenging ourselves to live the values, we can help set the tone. It is clear that Peterman, like myself, believes, while people are not born great leaders, through hard work and a determination to build a better self, anything is possible."

—Billy Elliott
President, Author Solutions

"Leadership to me is about managing the risk of the organization to ensure its success. There is a risk of growing too quickly and there is also a risk of being too complacent and being left behind. A good leader needs to be able to take an honest assessment of the organization's strengths and weaknesses and act decisively to set the best course. Chad illustrates in this book how his course of action that involves providing a platform for your people to grow and thrive leverages the strengths of the entire company, ultimately allowing growth for all."

—Eric Odmark
President, IMH Products

"Pete Peterman recognized early on that 'businesses grow when people do.' His investment in developing others while providing the opportunity for his staff to become masters of their craft, to work autonomously, and to do so with purpose has been a critical success factor to Peterman's growth. This book highlights the culture of servant leadership developed by Pete and carried on by his two boys, Chad and Tyler, that is readily displayed each day at Peterman Heating, Cooling & Plumbing."

—Drew Hettich
President, Wiers

"The number-one asset for any successful company is the people, the teams that get it done each and every day. Chad, his brother Tyler, and his family obviously not only believe this, *they live it*. In order to build a company you must care about the customer and instill in the team that, without the customer, the employees don't get paid and the company not only does not make money to support their people, their customers, and the business itself but they no longer have a business to run. 'Clients do not come first; employees come first. If you take care of your employees, they will take care of the clients.' This is a book that young and old can learn from. Congratulations on the tremendous success of Peterman Heating, Cooling & Plumbing and for understanding where you came from."

—Gary Halter
President, Indiana Oxygen Company

"If you are looking for a book that communicates the significance of company culture and positioning team members to succeed, this is the book for you. *You Can't Stop the Growth* underlines how essential it is to make employees number one, so that they can pass along excellent service to the customer. As home-service business owners are continually faced with the challenge of developing and retaining their talented team, Chad's philosophies bring real-world insights to lead a team to growth."

—Aaron Gaynor
Owner and CEO, The Eco Plumbers

"The Peterman company has been a long time valued Bryant Dealer. They have been a Bryant® Factory Authorized Dealer since 2012. Bryant and Habegger Corporation align with dedicated Bryant Factory Authorized Dealers who have made a commitment to excellence in their businesses through focus, determination, and leadership. A select few earn the distinction as a Bryant® Circle of Champions Award winner. The Peterman company has earned this prestigious award in 2018 and 2019. Bryant supports the Peterman family, their heritage, reputation and applauds Chad Peterman for bringing their story and values to life!"

—Margo Richter

Bryant Marketing Manager
Bryant Heating and Cooling Systems

You Can't Stop the Growth

Published by Advantage, Charleston, South Carolina.
Member of Advantage Media Group.

ADVANTAGE is a registered trademark, and the Advantage colophon is a trademark of Advantage Media Group, Inc.

Printed in the United States of America.

10 9 8 7 6 5 4 3 2 1

ISBN: 978-1-64225-158-6
LCCN: 2019917238

Book design by Matthew Morse.

This publication is designed to provide accurate and authoritative information in regard to the subject matter covered. It is sold with the understanding that the publisher is not engaged in rendering legal, accounting, or other professional services. If legal advice or other expert assistance is required, the services of a competent professional person should be sought.

Advantage Media Group is proud to be a part of the Tree Neutral® program. Tree Neutral offsets the number of trees consumed in the production and printing of this book by taking proactive steps such as planting trees in direct proportion to the number of trees used to print books. To learn more about Tree Neutral, please visit **www.treeneutral.com**.

Advantage Media Group is a publisher of business, self-improvement, and professional development books and online learning. We help entrepreneurs, business leaders, and professionals share their Stories, Passion, and Knowledge to help others Learn & Grow. Do you have a manuscript or book idea that you would like us to consider for publishing? Please visit **advantagefamily.com** or call **1.866.775.1696**.

*To the man who had a dream
and the woman who stood by his side to create a company
that will change the world.*

Contents

Introduction:

Can't Stop the Growth

I recently drove past the house where I grew up. I smiled and stopped the car when I saw the garage—the garage where my dad started our family business in 1986. As my mom tells the story, it was a hot, humid day in midsummer, and she was pregnant with me. Dad, who worked for a local heating and air-conditioning company, came home from work and suddenly announced that he was going to start his own company. My mom was stunned. It was a lean time, and with a baby on the way, she couldn't believe he was going to just quit his job to start up a new business. It took everything she had not to lose it at that point!

My dad went to technical school right out of high school. When he graduated in 1980, the country was in a recession, and no one was hiring. Every company he went to in the heating industry said they couldn't hire him because he needed experience, and he'd say, "Well, that's what I'm here to do: get experience!" It took a long time and a lot of shoe leather, but someone finally gave him an opportunity. He did a little bit of everything—installations and service work—and he picked it up quickly. More importantly, he enjoyed the work, and he loved meeting the customers and helping them with their problems. Pete Peterman had found his niche! He worked for that company for about five years. But by midsummer 1986, he felt as if he could do it better on his own, and thus the adventure began out of our garage.

Dad felt there was a better way for customers to get a furnace maintained or installed than what he saw while working in the industry for someone else—a better way than crossing your fingers, dialing a number in the phone book, and hoping the contractor doesn't take advantage of you. He knew that a lot of people can install, fix, or maintain a furnace, but customers have to be sure they can trust the companies they hire. He also thought that companies could treat their employees better.

> It's still the reason we're in business today: taking care of people, both our customers and our employees and their families.

Many companies are dedicated to the bottom line and to the people at the top of the employee pyramid. But some companies dedicate themselves both to growing great people and providing better service, and Peterman Heating, Cooling & Plumbing is one of them. Dad built our company on his dreams and his vision of working for himself while providing a good living for his family and his employees and their families.

It's still the reason we're in business today: taking care of people, both our customers and our employees and their families. Only today, we take care of more than 120 employees and thousands of satisfied customers!

The Peterman Story

Our company history is the foundation of our success today, so I want to go back to our garage in 1986 and tell that story. Dad had always wanted to do his own thing ever since he was a little kid, probably because his father had his own business (and still does today—an electrical company, and we work together on projects). Being an entrepreneur is in the blood. Dad knew it would take a lot of hard work and dedication, but with a growing family, he also knew it was his best chance to make a good living for his family. Working for someone else also exposed him to a work culture that he knew could be better, and he was determined that his company would be a better workplace for himself and, eventually, his employees. He jumped into his new business with both feet. Working out of that garage in 1986, he knew exactly what bills he had to pay each week—if he had $500 in bills, he needed to make $500 to take care of his family. So he did whatever he could to make ends meet, from drumming up business and running the service calls to getting his hands dirty with the technical work. He knew his customers needed a reason to call him again, a reason to remember his name, and that's how the business would grow and earn him a good reputation. He figured that a lot of people can have good technical skills and do good work, but not everyone understands how to take care of people, whether that's customers or employees. I guess Dad just had a knack for that kind of thing and was always a people person.

Dad worked out of the garage (and did some bookkeeping at the kitchen table) for the first full year with volunteer help from his sister, and he paid some cousins and a few guys from the neighborhood to help him out. Dad did pretty well in that first year (during which I was born), well enough to start hiring a few people, and soon he moved into the company's first commercial location. It wasn't big or pretty, but it got him started, and it was close to home. A few years later, Dad bought a more substantial facility and knew that he was committed for the long haul. The company continued growing, and the rat race of living from paycheck to paycheck to support his family became a thing of the past. At this point, he realized something that changed how he thought about his business: his employees had to provide for their families, too, and they relied on the company—and Pete Peterman—to do that. That thought could have scared Dad, but he embraced it instead, and he continued building his company on that premise. By the time I joined Peterman full time in 2011, we had around twenty employees.

I didn't plan to work in the family business because, truthfully, I just wasn't interested in it. Most guys in my position probably would have jumped into a family business during high school and certainly would have worked part time in their businesses during summer school breaks. My brother, Tyler, was different. He's always been mechanically inclined and well-suited to the business, and he wanted to work there right after high school. But my parents convinced him to go to college first. He graduated from the University of Indianapolis in December of 2012 with a degree in sports management, took one week off, and then joined Peterman. The company worked on many new construction projects at the time, and they put him in charge of a five-story apartment complex project in downtown Indianapolis called Artistry. I drive past Artistry a lot and think about how remarkable it is that a twenty-three-year-old kid ran a four-hundred-unit construction project.

I went to Wabash College to major in political science and history because I originally wanted to go to law school, but my dreams of a law career lasted about one semester. I didn't really know what I wanted to do. I stayed in those majors, graduated in 2009, and moved to Charlotte, North Carolina, for a sales job with a company that manufactured adhesives for many different industries. I traveled every week selling adhesives to the paper and packaging industry, and it was a great job for a guy fresh out of college with no responsibilities whatsoever. I had a little money in my pocket and was really just getting my feet wet in the real world. I stayed with that company for two years when something happened that changed how I felt about my family's business.

My first boss challenged me to learn as much as I could about business, and I've always been eager to learn, so I started reading general business books on topics such as leadership and improving yourself. I can admit now that the real reason I wasn't interested in the family business is that it had always intimidated me—not the business side of it, but the technical aspect. Then reading all of those business books somehow got me curious about what Dad was doing and what was going on in the company, and I realized that I no longer saw Peterman as a technical company and instead started seeing it as a business. In the summer of 2011, I dived into the company's marketing, budgets, projections, and other business areas. I still lived in Charlotte, but I just started getting involved with different aspects of the company that I could work with remotely. The first thing I did (without any real background in it) was rebuild our entire website, and then I was hooked. I moved back to Indianapolis in the fall of 2011 to work at Peterman full time and start business school for a master's degree.

Because we were a smaller company, the big question around the office then was "What's he going to do?" Everyone knew I wouldn't be a service technician or an installer. The first thing I did was rebuild our website—I'd tried looking us up on Google and had a hard time finding us, so I knew there was work to do on our site. Then I did what I knew at the time: I jumped into the sales and marketing side, learning from our only salesperson how to do estimates, what equipment we sold, and how to sell it. And then he quit, just as summer was heating up and it was going to get really, really hot in Indianapolis. Dad said to me, "You're all we've got to sell equipment now, so go get 'em!" The company no longer intimidated me, and I took on more than just sales, overseeing the service department along with all of the marketing, some operations, and some back-office functions. At this point, I was really just getting my feet wet, and it was a blessing for me to be able to experience literally all sides of the business.

The next couple of years were busy—I worked and went to school at night, and we started our plumbing division during this time. I was learning both at school and on the job. The great thing about a small business is that you get to touch everything, and I've done literally everything in the business. But the big changes in the business and in my brother and me as leaders happened when the real source of our company's growth became clear to us.

Growth Is All about Our People

During my first five years with the company, as Dad handed more responsibility over to Tyler and me, he cautioned us not to grow too fast. Dad's vision of taking care of both our customers and our employees and their families was different, and because it was so different from the norm in our industry, he's always been cautious about growth. We took his advice at first because we really didn't have any other basis to form our own opinions about how we should do it. So we turned our attention inward to focus on our employees— finding the best people, committing to their growth, and making it our mission to create the best work culture that we could. The company was already a great place to work, and we knew that working at Peterman had a lot of great perks and advantages, but we also felt we could do a better job of telling others about it. As we built up our recruitment brand, we started to attract exceptionally good people who were motivated to grow their careers, improve, and get to the next level.

At Peterman, we connected growth to everybody winning—both the employees and the company. Growth is often associated with words like "headache" and the idea that having more people means more problems and issues. I think that often comes from management growing for

> The more our employees grew individually, the more the business grew, and we soon saw that in the end, the pace of growth was really up to the employees.

their own personal reasons, and it's what causes employees to fear growth and not buy in to a company's growth plans. But we made sure our people understood that growth is good for everyone—opportunities open for them if we're growing because as we do more work, we need more people, and therefore management positions and field supervisor positions open up; pay rates increase, and a company can give employees more incentives. Adding new departments opens even more opportunities, especially for those who want to get in on the ground floor of something new. We gave them every opportunity to improve themselves personally and professionally, and they took those opportunities. The more our employees grew individually, the more the business grew, and we soon saw that in the end, the pace of growth was really up to the employees.

Empowering People to Succeed

Today, I'm the president of Peterman Heating, Cooling & Plumbing, and the company employs more than 120 people. We've outgrown our facility after eighteen years and are building a new one that's about three times as big as our current building.

Peterman Heating, Cooling & Plumbing has transformed from a business to a vehicle that affects people's lives in positive ways. I believe that our growth and success come from a special culture we created that not only draws people to work here but keeps them here—we have a very low turnover rate compared with the rest of our industry. A company's culture is built on its core values, and for us, that didn't mean building nap rooms or bringing in ping-pong tables like the Silicon Valley software companies do. Our culture centers on empowering our people to succeed. It's built on caring about each and every person and the belief that everyone should be treated fairly, whether they're a rock-star salesperson or a new employee coming in who doesn't know very much about the business or the industry. When we show how much we care, employees understand that the company as a whole cares about them. That's when they'll run through walls for you and will do anything they can to help you accomplish the company's vision through their own career goals.

To be frank, the trades are often a person's last resort if they didn't do well in school. You sometimes see people in the trades who have never dreamed, or if they did, someone along the way crushed those dreams, and they're afraid to ever dream again. I believe that instilling hope, care, and compassion in the life of someone like that will start them dreaming again, setting goals, and accomplishing things—and then you have to recognize them for it. To me, this is why Peterman's culture is so special. We provide a place our employees can call home, a place where our plumbers, heating technicians, installers, salespeople, or whatever they may be can show off their skills to the world. We don't want to hold anyone back—quite the contrary. We don't put limits on anyone. Instead, we say, "As long as we grow, there's a place for you."

Dad was always taking care of people in one way or another, and the people who worked for him respected him. Dad's still involved in the business, but I still remember the day he told us not to grow too fast (this was *after* we'd already grown a lot), and I just shook my head.

"Dad, I *can't* stop it. When you get the culture right and you find great people, *they* are growing the business, and they don't want to stop improving. I'm just here to give them a platform to help them be successful. I can't stop them from wanting to get better and be better. I can't stop the growth!"

That idea—you can't stop the growth if you hire the right people and empower them to succeed—is why I wrote this book. Our company is successful and still growing, and I want to share how we've done that through the years. I think a lot of companies might want to use the lessons we've learned as we grew and implement some of our strategies. Customers, too, can learn something from our experience that can help them hire companies they can trust. We've all heard horror stories about contractors who take advantage of customers, and we're showing them it's not the only way to do business. But my true hope for this book is that whenever a customer asks one of our employees what makes us different, he or she can give the customer a copy and say, "Here's what makes us different. We really are doing something special here—this is all about how we do it and why we do it."

Chapter 1:

Treat Your Team Members as Number One

We wanted you to know that you, Jay, and Tony, and all of the team members and the company itself once again hit a walk-off grand slam. Every person who came to our home was professional, very polite, took time to explain the work they performed, and asked if we had any questions. This was not just one or two team members, but all of them. From my first encounter with Peterman in the early 1980s, I believe, Pete had his shop on Bethel Avenue in Beech Grove and may have had one or two employees. I called one very cold winter afternoon because the furnace would not light. Your dad told me he would be leaving the shop in about an hour and would stop by the house, which was about a half a block from the shop. The thermocouple was dirty and needed cleaning; it was blown out. He took time to show me how to disconnect and clean the thermocouple, eliminating the need for future service calls. He charged me nothing, smiled, shook my hand, and told my wife and me to have a good night. Today, the business has grown, but the owner's personality has passed down to all of the employees with whom I have had the pleasure of dealing. Again, thank you!

—Satisfied customer

Have you ever worked for a company where you knew some of your coworkers when you saw them, but you didn't know their names? You might walk past someone in the hallway and know the face, say "hello" to the person, but you just didn't know their name. That doesn't happen at Peterman. We all know and support each other—every employee, from leadership to the newest team member—and all employees know that they're an important part of the company. Our culture at Peterman is one of mutual caring, support, and respect, and it's the basis for how our employees treat our customers. If team members feel important and respected, they'll make the customer feel important and respected too. Believe me, customers can tell the difference.

Putting Employees First and the Company Last

Many companies focus strictly on revenue and hope that their employees will produce it, and then they reward the employees last. I think those companies have it backward. If you're in leadership, it seems counterintuitive to not put the company first and want to increase revenue, yet we've found that treating team members well and putting them first is the best way to increase revenue through excellent customer service. The company wins in the end, but it *does* win. This idea grew out of our goal of making Peterman the best place that any of our people have ever worked. Obviously, we need to make a profit to stay in business. But when you think about how companies like ours really create revenue, it becomes clear how the revenue-first thinking is backward.

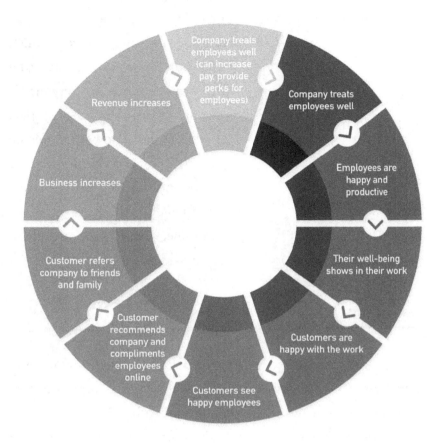

A company creates revenue through providing excellent service, growing its customer base, and keeping current customers happy. The company's employees accomplish those things by doing their best work. We proved that supporting our employees and making them number one results in them doing their best work. They provide excellent service that makes our customers happy and gives them real value for their money—this keeps our customers coming back to us when they need products and service, and they refer their friends, families, and neighbors to us. As our business grows, our revenue increases because our employees did their best work. We can pay employees (because we've collected money) and pay them well, and we provide perks and benefits that many companies in our industry can't or simply won't provide. Our employees are happy, and the pay and benefits allow us to recruit more high-quality employees, which feeds our culture. It's a cycle and a win-win situation for everyone. If revenue-first thinking puts employees last, how can anyone possibly win? Clearly, the revenue will be there as long as employees are first and the company creates an atmosphere that supports them and makes them feel supported.

> Clearly, the revenue will be there as long as employees are first and the company creates an atmosphere that supports them and makes them feel supported.

Caring Starts with Leadership

A culture of caring, support, and mutual respect starts with leadership showing all employees that they're number one. So where do you start to build such a culture? I don't advise giving everyone in the office a Segway or building swimming pools like so many of the giant technology companies do. That's not what culture is really about. Rather it's caring about people—whether they're a rock-star salesperson or a new employee coming with little knowledge or experience—and making sure they know that everyone will be treated fairly, and everyone should care about each other. At Peterman, we committed to building a culture of caring in which all employees feel that the company puts them first. We used the following five strategies to build that culture:

- Commit to knowing each employee as a person.
- Encourage employees to know each other.
- Cultivate an atmosphere of one team: we're all in this together.
- Give employees tangible benefits to show that you care.
- Understand how you and your company affect people's lives.

In the next sections, I'll describe how we implemented these strategies into a cohesive company culture that fuels our growth and delivers the best service to our customers.

Employees Aren't Just a Number

I saw an article once titled, "Management Is 10 Percent Work and 90 Percent People," and I completely agree with that thought. Management is about getting the job done through other people, and you have to know those people if you want to motivate them and make them happy to come to work every day. I admit that as our company grows, it becomes a bit harder to know every employee. But that just means that we in leadership have to try harder to get to know everyone. One way we accomplish this is by meeting people when they are first hired on. Either my brother is or I am involved in nearly every interview for an open job position at Peterman. We learn a lot about the applicant, the type of people we're attracting, and what's going on in the rest of our industry, but we also want to make sure the person will fit into our company culture. I think that's one of the biggest things companies overlook. It's our job as the leaders to attract the best and create an atmosphere in which employees feel they're part of a group of top performers. I make it a point to meet as many prospective employees as possible, and I tell each person what everyone who already works here knows: you're not just a number at Peterman, and though I might not interact with you every day, I'm going to know your name and something about you, no matter how many people we hire.

Another strategy we use is a monthly breakfast for new employees hired in that month. It's only for the new hires and my brother and me. This relaxed atmosphere helps tear down the invisible wall between employees and leadership right at the start by giving new hires a chance to talk with leadership one on one. We don't want employees to be afraid to talk with us just because we're the owners. Leaders in many companies say they have open-door policies, but if they haven't done anything to make employees feel truly welcome to walk through that door and talk with them, the policy doesn't mean anything. My door is always open for employees, and our employees know they're welcome to walk through it. They understand that the company as a whole cares about them, and when they know that, they'll run through walls for you, so to speak. They'll do anything in their power to help you accomplish the company's vision through their own career goals.

I've found that people enjoy getting to know us, and it's refreshing because I don't think other companies make it as easy to get to know leadership and communicate well with them. Employees find that there's less pressure and they can just be themselves, and ultimately, that's who we want them to be for the customers. We hire our people for a reason—because they have certain skills or we think they have a lot of potential. We want them to be who they are, which makes them happier and is good for the customers too.

Bring Employees Together

Leadership should encourage employees to know each other, too, and every day, we do our best to get everyone to intermingle in some way. One of the best places to do this is at our monthly company meetings. We set up tables and make seating arrangements so that only two people per department are at a table. This way, team members will meet different people in the company they normally don't see every day, and it keeps little cliques from forming by department. It's also a good way for people in one department to learn about how other departments function daily, and that can help everyone's work go more smoothly. For example, one department might learn about issues that another department faces, and they can start talking about those issues and possibly come up with solutions to make the workflow better. They get involved with each other, which often leads to better working relationships because they're communicating in a relaxed, social way. It's important for the company to keep communication channels like that open.

Holding company events is another way we bring people together, including their families. Our annual holiday or Christmas party is our biggest event. Many people dread going to their company Christmas party—people just seem to dread it and don't want to go for a lot of reasons. You often hear people say of company events, "I work with those people for eight hours a day—I don't want to have to go there on a Saturday or after hours and be with them again!" At Peterman, the Christmas party is probably our biggest event, and everyone gets really get excited about it. I know that we're doing something right because attendance at these parties is about 96 percent.

Every day, I see our people willing to help one another. Our experienced people are always willing to step up and help the younger people who need training. Those with less experience don't have to feel like they're out there all alone because someone who's done this before is only a phone call away. Most people in our industry haven't had this kind of work experience before. It takes time to build a culture of caring, and many companies don't want to take the time needed to grow that culture slowly. But it's truly worth it to invest in employees in this way. At Peterman, our employees protect our reputation, our work, and our name for two reasons: first and foremost, we're all in this together, and second, they know there's nothing else like this out there. Our team members *are* Peterman. They wear the name on their shirts, and that's who they are.

We're All in This Together

When you know your employees as people, it's easier to understand what they want and need and what motivates them. Then you can come up with simple practices that can be highly effective in pulling people together as teams that care and support each other. As leaders, we care about our employees and support them, and we set the example for everyone. My brother and I set the tone for our company: we're all in this together. We believe that feeling starts at the top, and we have to set the example because our employees see how we behave toward everyone. I think that treating people well and with respect is contagious. I'm sure that I've never yelled or screamed at anybody if

> They wear the name on their shirts, and that's who they are.

something went wrong on the job. No one shows to work up wanting to do a bad job, and sometimes things just go wrong. I figure that as leaders, we need to take ownership for the situation and understand that when something goes wrong, it's more likely because we haven't communicated what needs to be done.

Employees know that if we're all in this together, it means they're never on their own at Peterman. Someone is always willing to help you when you have a problem. For example, our people working out in the field will undoubtedly run into problems and need to call the office for help. When they do, they know that the person they call will actually help them instead of belittling them for not being able to solve the crisis on their own. I've heard stories about field technicians from other companies being told, "Just go on YouTube; you can figure it out!" Would your customers be comfortable with technicians who turned to YouTube to solve their problems? That doesn't happen at Peterman. Our employees all have different skills, and if we put them all together, we can solve many problems for our customers. Everyone in our company understands an important fact: I can't do my job without you, and you can't do your job without me. It benefits all of us if we help each other.

Benefits for Employees That Benefit Everyone

Building a supportive company culture includes providing employees with programs and benefits that have real value for them. This is why nap rooms and ping-pong tables don't fall into this category. Real value for employees means something that helps them on the job or in their personal lives and helps them build for the future for themselves and their families. It's an investment for the company, but we're investing in the employees. Going back to the revenue cycle, we feel the company benefits in the end.

We've rolled out several programs in recent years that our employees appreciate. Most companies in our industry don't provide benefits like these, which makes Peterman an attractive employer. We've already seen the positive impact these benefits have on our employees, so I'll describe several as examples of what companies can to show employees that they care and build a strong, supportive culture.

Guaranteed 40 Program

This program is rather unique in our industry, so it's a real standout when recruiting and is very popular with our employees. Our heating, ventilation, and air-conditioning installation department operates somewhat seasonally. Work can be slow depending on the time of year and weather, which means that our installers have unpredictable hours that can make it very difficult to budget for personal expenses, like the car payment, mortgage, utility bills, food, and so on. We know that these seasonal slowdowns are hard on people, and it didn't sit well with us. We don't want our people to feel stressed out and possibly carry the weight of a tough financial situation when they're trying to be their best for our customers. So we created a program called Guaranteed 40, which guarantees that every installer will be paid for forty hours of work, regardless of how many hours they actually work.

For example, an installer might work only twenty-five hours during a slow week, but he or she will still be paid for forty hours. However, if the installer works fifty hours in a busy week, he or she is paid for fifty hours. There's no downside for team members—they no longer have to worry about unpredictable pay schedules, they can manage their personal budgets without stress, regardless of the weather, and they know they can take care of their families without the uncertainty of unsteady work. The customer also benefits because the installation crew isn't concerned about their personal finances and can focus only on installing the customer's new system. Our company wins because we can retain our great people and offer them an amazing benefit.

Health Insurance

We recently rolled out a new health insurance package that has no deductible, which is a very nice benefit for employees. This is one of those benefits that helps eliminate stress. Our employees aren't staring at a huge deductible figure and crossing their fingers, hoping that no one gets sick in their families.

Classes and Seminars

We believe that the people who are going to take the company to the next level will come from within the company, and to that end, we want to give our employees opportunities to learn and grow. We send employees to training and offer several classes here at our facility. For example, I teach a series of classes every other Saturday called Our Future Series. It's a four-module course on leadership, personal productivity, and business acumen, and it's open to everyone in the company. This is especially popular with employees who typically wouldn't have access to this type of training, like a technician who's out in a truck all day. We have a lot of capable people in our company who might want to become managers one day or might just want to improve their personal lives, and I want to make sure that they have the resources needed to improve and be their best.

Tools

An important benefit for our employees in the field is our tool account program. Our employees in the trades have to have tools to do their jobs, and their tools can be costly for them. Our tool account gives each technician up to $600 a year to buy tools and other equipment they need for the job. We're proud of this program and consider it one of our best. I've checked around the industry to see if I could find another similar program, and I haven't yet found any that are better than ours.

Birthday Paid Holiday

This is more of a fun benefit that's definitely an employee favorite. Everybody here gets their birthday off as a paid holiday. Even if the birthday falls on a weekend, they still get a paid holiday off—Friday if the birthday is on a Saturday, Monday if it's on a Sunday. Everyone loves being able to take off work on their birthdays and spend the day with their families.

These are just a few examples of what makes Peterman different. Companies that want to start creating a better work culture can use some of these strategies or develop some of their own based on knowing their employees as people. I think the most important thing to think about is how whatever you're doing will affect your employees' lives both at work and at home.

Affecting Employees' Lives

How do we as employers affect people and their lives? I've thought about this question a lot. Our team members are with us for forty hours a week, and the rest of the time, they're raising their kids, getting them through high school and into college, and helping them with difficult situations. It would be wonderful if people could leave work every day and leave every aspect of work behind at the office, but that rarely happens. People usually take the problems, attitudes, stresses, and general feelings of their workplaces home with them, and it affects their families and life at home.

Although our job as a company is to support our employees while they're working, I think a greater purpose is to provide a good workplace environment, one that they love and won't affect them negatively after they leave each day. We don't want our employees to take home a lot of negativity. I'd rather they have careers that make them proud and make them good examples for their children and even their spouses. People who work at Peterman are on fire, even after a tough day. They're excited to get to their kids' baseball games or plays or recitals, but more importantly, their kids can see that they love what they do—that they love their lives.

To me, that's when our impact extends from our employees to many more people: it goes to their families, too, and especially to our customers, whose lives are affected positively through the service we provide. I've heard our employees' spouses say that they're grateful for this place and how much their spouses love what they do. I'm proud that we have that effect on people, because if our only impact came from just producing revenue for the company, I'd feel like I'm doing a disservice to those people.

If you love what you do and you love the people working with you, that perspective on life is going to carry over into your personal life. I want to reach people on a level that makes them better parents because working at Peterman is a positive environment that doesn't send them home disgruntled each day. Employees tell me they're excited to talk about their workdays when they get home, and their kids know they love their jobs. This is an example of what a company having a larger purpose means. Children who see what a work environment can be might one day say, "Mom and Dad loved where they work. I want to find a place where I love to work, and I won't tolerate anything less."

These strategies and programs aren't for companies that believe the sole focus of the business is to serve the leader, or for the owner who looks for every way to trim overhead to create slightly better margins. The Peterman way is to invest in intangible things and spend money on our people's well-being. They also aren't for companies that focus solely on the bottom line or view each employee as just a number whose position is merely a means to an end. There's nothing wrong with a bottom-line focus, and great companies have been built using this method, but it's not our philosophy. We believe that company owners should try to meet and get to know each team member as an individual—a person with unique characteristics and personality, standing in the community, likes and dislikes, and wants and needs. Employees aren't just numbers, and that's what makes the Peterman philosophy compelling.

Chapter 2:

Lead Yourself

I would recommend Peterman Heating, Cooling & Plumbing without hesitation. From first contact with Ashley to when John came out to look at my plumbing issues, they were professional, friendly, and informative. Ashley was able to schedule the service call for the plumbing that day and also worked with me to set up a furnace tune-up for while I was off work. Logan was the furnace technician and was professional and helpful and able to give me some suggestions for other work I would like to get done in the future. John was awesome and worked with me to provide the best solutions to the work I needed done as well as quickly coordinate with a company to deal with water damage that was found. Bailey and John came the first day and completed the work that could be done that day. After the work was completed on one of the issues, it turned out that it would need more work to correct the problem (I have very old pipes). After giving me some options, John came back the next day and completed what needed to be done. Total satisfaction with the work done by all along with the best customer service ever! Professional, helpful, and friendly with top notch work! I 100 percent recommend this company!

—Kerri S.

I had to learn to be a leader because it didn't come naturally to me. When I joined the family business, I stepped in and started doing whatever I could, which involved some leadership. But I had to learn a lot more about the business and about myself before I could evolve into a larger leadership role. Honestly, at first, I was flying by the seat of my pants as a leader. I often asked myself, "What's a leader supposed to do? What's the difference between a manager and a leader?" Now that I had this responsibility, I didn't know what I was going to do with it. I wasn't sure if I had enough confidence in myself. So I did what I always do: I turned to books.

I'm an avid reader. I typically read a book a week from many different genres, not just business books. You probably wonder where I find the time to read a book a week with a business to run and a personal life to live. It's not that I find the time, but rather I make the time. I've committed to quiet time by myself every day to just read, write, and learn. At first, I did this to find answers to the dozens of questions swirling in my head about how I could be a good leader. But I also realized that in doing so, I was taking charge of my own development, motivating myself, even managing my own behavior. I was holding myself accountable to my own values, beliefs, and goals. These are all things I would eventually lead others to do, so in effect, I was leading myself first so that I could lead others better.

I believe that all leaders should lead themselves first. If you have bad habits, aren't taking responsibility for yourself, and aren't willing to put in the work—and your employees see this—you're going to have a hard time getting others to believe in you, often because what they see is you not believing in yourself. Through my own experience, I've found five important things that leaders can do to lead themselves and become the best examples for their employees that they can be.

1. Take responsibility for yourself.
2. Commit to personal development.
3. Develop your emotional intelligence.
4. Share your knowledge with others.
5. Be grateful and serve others.

Take Responsibility for Yourself

I recall that I didn't know my true purpose as a leader or fully understand my role when I first joined the company. I thought that Peterman's mission was to install furnaces and fix plumbing. This was during the time that we were cautious about growing too fast and had changed the focus of the business from revenue to our people and our customers. I understood then that my purpose tied directly to the company's mission of creating a remarkable place for people to work and having a positive effect on their lives. I accepted this purpose because it connected perfectly with my personal purpose. Your true purpose as a leader will emerge as you discover and evolve your company's larger mission.

Understanding my role meant knowing the difference between managers and leaders, and it's a big difference. We didn't need leaders when the business was small and we had only about fifteen people working for us. We needed only managers who oversaw the work scheduled for the day. But when my dad started to step away from his leadership role, we needed to change from a group of managers to actual leaders.

Managers concentrate on directing people to do the work—telling them what work is scheduled for the day, making sure everyone knows what they need to do, and ensuring they do it correctly, even telling them exactly how to do it. Leaders, however, focus on what matters to the company and its people and why it matters, and they influence people in many ways, both personally and professionally. They understand the company's vision, exemplify it, live it every day, and they give people something to believe in. When I understood the difference, it was a bit daunting, but I remembered that I'd been in leadership positions before in my life. As an athlete, I was captain of my teams, and in that sense, being a leader came naturally. I interpreted the coach telling me, "Go be a leader" to mean that I should play hard and say encouraging things to my teammates—and that was a good interpretation. Playing hard gave them an example to follow, and saying encouraging things showed I believed in them and cared about them. I suppose I could say that I was my own best influence in my early leadership days, but as the company grew, I knew I needed much more. My dad, of course, was a big influence on me. But my dad and I are two different people. I had to find my own way, and because I've always been a learner, my first instinct was to turn to books and commit to finding my own leadership style.

> Leaders inspire people. Employees are always watching their leaders and, whether or not they realize it, they look to their leaders as examples.

Set the Example

Leaders inspire people. Employees are always watching their leaders and, whether or not they realize it, they look to their leaders as examples. Yet many leaders often believe that rules don't apply to them—they come into work late and leave early, they're always late for meetings and aren't prepared, they take two- or three-hour lunch breaks, or they skip work to play golf. How can such a leader possibly inspire anyone? They're certainly not setting a good example.

Leading by example is a big part of my leadership style. Our people need to see me working, giving it my all, going shoulder to shoulder with them into battle because we're going to win today for the customers, for ourselves, and for the company. They know that even though I work in an office most of the time, I can't do my job without them, and they can't do their jobs without me—that's what makes us a team. We depend on one another. I think that some leaders get that backward by thinking that everybody in their organization is there to serve them just because they're in charge. "You guys go do the work and then report back." I see it differently. I'm not too good for any task. My brother and I were both sweeping the floor in the warehouse not long ago. It tells people that everybody does their part and that we're a team, no matter what our official titles might be—and that's how great things are accomplished.

Our employees need to see leadership holding themselves accountable when things go wrong. Too many times, I hear about companies that fire people because they didn't hit some target number of sales or jobs completed without finding out why this happened. Yes, a business has to make money, but there's also a point where you as the leader have to look inside and ask yourself why this person is struggling. Instead of blaming the person, it's a leader's responsibility to care enough to find out why there's a problem and then help to fix it. Maybe you didn't train him or her enough or give the right information, or maybe it's an issue at home, a lack of confidence, or lack of practice. Whatever it is, you as the leader need to get to the bottom of it and understand where you can help that person.

When you do this, it sets the example for how everyone behaves when things go wrong.

I believe that leaders who take responsibility for themselves and hold themselves accountable are the foundation of a great workplace culture. Leaders must do these things to be good examples and inspire others.

Commit to Personal Development

The term "personal development" can have many meanings. To me, it means the activities I do to improve myself as a person and a leader. I don't follow someone else's program because personal development is, well, personal. You have to know yourself and be able to look at yourself objectively to know where you need improvement, and then you find ways to learn and make improvements that will work for you. What I do for my own personal development might not work for others. I can only relate what I do and confirm that my strategies have worked well for me over the years.

I read many books about mindset, which psychologists say is a way of thinking, the sum of your thoughts and beliefs that affects how you think, what you feel, and what you do. As a leader, your mindset is so important because others look to you as an example. In the workplace, your mindset can and will become your employees' mindset, and mindset is a big part of how you view challenges and cope with them. This is why I believe it's crucial to train your mind to be positive. As a leader and an entrepreneur, you face a lot of challenges and problems daily, even hourly. These are problems to solve, not the end of the world, and leaders are like firefighters always putting out fires. With a positive mindset, you believe there's always a solution, and people feed off that. When people come to me with a big problem, I always tell them, "Well, we've been in business for nearly thirty-three years, and we've always figured out the answers to the problems. I have no doubt we'll figure this one out too." There's a lot of confidence in that, too, and it's all part of a positive mindset.

I do my best when my days are well structured, and I attribute how I structure my day to my dad. He woke up at the same time every day for thirty-three years and went to work. His philosophy was, "You have to get up, and you have to go work hard." He influenced me very early in my life to show up, be prepared, and get your work done, and I feel that's how I can be most successful for myself and for our people. Having played sports all my life, I approach every day as if I'm preparing for a game. If running the business is the game, I need to prepare before I start my workday. Luckily, I've always been a morning person. Mornings are the best time for me to use my brain-power because my brain shuts off at the end of the day after work. My morning routine, which I follow strictly every day, is my time for personal development and preparing for the game, and it's probably the most powerful part of my day. It starts early at 3:00 a.m. To get my day going at that time, I usually go to bed by 10:00 p.m. at the latest. Here's what I do in the first few hours after awakening:

- 3:00 a.m.—I spend one hour learning by reading and listening to podcasts on topics such as mindset, leadership techniques, and how to create work culture.
- 4:00 a.m.—I spend the next forty-five minutes thinking about a big problem or the possibility of implementing something new at work. It's good to do this after reading for a couple of hours because I'm primed with ideas and can often come up with solutions I might not have thought about before.
- 4:45 a.m.—I start journaling for about a half hour, and it's an important part of my routine. I use three separate journals,

one of which relates only to business. I jot down ideas I come across in my reading, and it's a good resource for me throughout my day, especially when I'm preparing material for our leadership classes.

- 5:15 a.m.—Breakfast
- 5:30 a.m.—I wake up my daughter, and by this time, I'm ready to go with the rest of my day. I'm excited to see her and to get the day started.
- 6:30 a.m.—I start my day at work.

I look forward to my morning routine because it primes me to be the leader that I need to be, and it helps me grow. I think that as leaders, we often forget about ourselves and don't take the time we need to work on ourselves. If we're going to be great for other people and lift other people up, we must continue to grow ourselves. As busy as we are, we must find and make time for ourselves to grow. Those early-morning hours are for me and me alone, and I make the most of them.

As I outlined my routine, I mentioned only my business journal, but my other two journals are just as important because they focus on life in general. One of them is for my daughter, and I write in it first, usually one page a day of life advice, things I've learned, and anything else I want to tell her. I started keeping this journal before she was born, and I hope the things I write to her will help and guide her in life when she's old enough to read and understand it. Writing to her helps me, too, by grounding me in what life is truly all about. If I have a stressful day coming up, or one filled with meetings that I don't really want to attend, writing to my daughter always reminds me that my overall my duty today is to affect somebody in a positive way.

Then I write in my own journal. I always start out by listing three things for which I'm grateful because it grounds me and makes me feel that no matter what happens that day, everything will be all right. Life is good, and we need to remind ourselves of that every day, especially when tough situations come up. We're all very blessed to be where we are, to be doing what we do. The rest of my journal writing flows from there. Again, I'm grounding myself in what *is*—what's important about what I'm doing, why I'm doing it, and all the things I'm grateful for. I think that as a leader of a growing company, it becomes easier to be caught up in the headaches and lose what you're all about as a person, and you start wondering, "Why am I here?" So I always start with being grateful for three things. After that, I find myself getting pumped up for the day, even on those mornings we all have when you wake and just want to go back to sleep. When I finish writing, I know it's going to be a great day.

FOUR PERSONAL DEVELOPMENT STEPS

- Find yourself. How do you do that? Figure out how to travel on your own journey of personal discovery. I do it through reading and learning. You might find other ways to discover what you really want to do in life—what you truly want to do versus "Well, this is my career." This is the fun part because once you figure that out, you'll never stop living your mission.

- Discover what's important to you. Understanding what you're all about and knowing what's important to you become the vision for your business, something larger that everyone who works for you can believe in and stand behind. This is why entrepreneurs start businesses in the first place.

- Learn from others and allow influences. There's a world of material out there on successful businesses, the people who led them to success, and how they did it. Read and learn, but be sure to do so within your own experiences. There's a big difference between learning from someone (and being influenced by someone) and copying what they do. The martial artist Bruce Lee wrote something in the dedication to his book that's relevant to this: "Research your own experience; absorb what is useful, reject what is useless, and add what is essentially your own."

- Be yourself. Too many people try to run a business like somebody else does, but that's not you. This relates directly to the previous point. If how you lead is mimicking someone else and doesn't come from within you, people will see right through that. You have to do it your way, and your way will emerge as you continue learning and growing.

Develop Your Emotional Intelligence

Emotional intelligence means being smart about feelings, both yours and those of the people around you. Developing your emotional intelligence helps you to manage your own emotions and the emotions of others. This leadership skill is so important to a company's culture and the example a leader sets because it relates directly to how people treat each other. Leaders need to keep people in emotional balance, so managing high-pressure and emotional situations is something we cover in our leadership training at Peterman.

We teach people that everyone's going to make mistakes, period, and getting angry, pointing fingers, and assigning blame doesn't solve the problem or lead to positive results. In our industry, the jobs can be difficult sometimes, and bad things are going to happen. If people expect that nothing bad is ever going to happen, they're probably going to be disappointed many times. When a big problem arises, leaders need to keep a cool head, especially if everyone around them is losing their cool. Instead of yelling and screaming at people, leaders should be supportive and show everyone that they solve problems by using what's in their heads and tool bags.

I think an emotionally intelligent leader understands the pulse of the organization. They understand that you need all types of people to help move your organization forward, and it's important to know your people well enough to know how you need to interact with each person and how to act yourself in different situations. Sometimes, you need to be an all-inspiring leader who gives an inspiring speech that gets people charged up and motivated, but other times, you just need to care about one person and his or her situation. For example, you need to keep your own emotions in check if someone is struggling and affecting the organization, and dig into what's going on in that person's life instead. Ask the person what's wrong and whether you can do something to help. Maybe it's a family issue; maybe they don't feel well, or it could be something else. But an emotionally intelligent leader acts rather than reacts.

A leader often needs to act differently depending on whom you're leading. All people respond differently to situations, so it's up to you to understand when you need to ask questions, when you need to provide guidance, and when you should let people figure things out on their own. Being sensitive to emotional signals from within yourself and from others in your organization makes you a better leader. Fortunately, you can hone these skills, and I've learned several ways to do this.

FOUR WAYS TO DEVELOP YOUR EMOTIONAL INTELLIGENCE

- Always be positive. As a leader, if you have a negative attitude, you only open the door for your team members to be negative, too, and I've rarely seen negative attitudes solve problems. Keeping a positive attitude makes it easier to control your own emotions and to set that good example for your teams.

- Adapt to situations. This doesn't mean having different personalities, but rather knowing how you can help in a particular situation, and often that depends on who's involved. Again, this requires you to know enough about each person so that you can interact with them effectively on an individual level.

- Remember that everyone is equal. I like to say that the organization chart at Peterman is flat, meaning that all employees—including me—are on the same level. I firmly believe that at the end of the day, leaders are no better than the lowest person on the totem pole. Of course, a chain of command's necessary to keep the company running smoothly. But it's clear to everyone that our company isn't a dictatorship. Leaders can't do their jobs if they don't have everyone else's buy-in. They need to cultivate the idea that everyone is in this together.

- Give everyone something to believe in. They *need* something to believe in, and leaders are in charge of creating that vision—whatever it might be in your company. Employees will be top performers when you give them something to believe in that's bigger than they are, but "bigger than they are" doesn't mean serving you. It means doing something much bigger than what they're capable of doing on their own, something they can do because they're part of your team.

Share Your Knowledge

In November 2018, we decided that it was time for us to start training our own leaders because I believe the future leaders of our company probably work for us right now. Our company is much larger than many in our industry, so we need more leaders than smaller companies do. I remember thinking early one morning as I was reading that I'm not truly benefiting the organization if I don't teach our people what I'm learning every day. To me, that makes whatever book I'm reading extremely powerful because it can affect many more people than just me. The training is part of our commitment to our people and my commitment to sharing knowledge.

I designed the entire program, taking inspiration from the books, articles, and podcasts I study in my morning routine. I teach the two-hour class myself every other Saturday, and it's broken into thirty-minute modules on topics such as personal development, leadership, business acumen, and peak performance. Attendance is voluntary and open to anyone who wants to attend from the top to the bottom of the company—leaders, managers, customer service representatives, technicians, and parts runners attend. The course is ongoing as long as our people want to keep learning.

This might seem like a lot of extra work for me beyond what I have to do every day, but I don't see it that way. I think teaching, sharing knowledge, and lifting people up are part of my duties as a leader. Having to come up with new material constantly puts a little bit of pressure on me, but it's good pressure because it holds me accountable to learn and keep learning. I'm extremely passionate about this training and providing our people with this benefit that's somewhat uncommon in our industry.

Along with sharing knowledge, I make sure to share opportunities to gain knowledge by sending our people to other training programs besides our in-house courses. I find classes all over the country on subjects such as best customer service practices, management practices, and marketing that will help our employees provide the best service possible to our customers. For example, the customer service training is a three-day course that teaches how to run a service call effectively and efficiently. I think that providing educational opportunities really shows employees that we care enough to invest in them and their futures, and it's investing in the company's future too. If, as a business owner, you don't feel you have the ability or can take the time to create your own training, you can probably find plenty of outside educational opportunities for your people that will be worth the investment.

Be Grateful and Serve Others

Leadership is about serving others, and I think of myself as a servant leader. I understand that, as a leader, I have a wonderful opportunity to serve others and affect their lives, and that means both our employees and our customers. I'm grateful for the responsibility, and I embrace it. Every morning when I journal, I list three things that

I'm grateful for, and I know I've listed "the opportunity to affect people's lives" more than once because it's so important and powerful.

One thing I've learned about gratitude is that you have to show it. I can write about how grateful I am for our employees and customers all I want, but they won't know about it unless I show it. I think it's easy to

> I understand that, as a leader, I have a wonderful opportunity to serve others and affect their lives, and that means both our employees and our customers.

become selfish in business. Entrepreneurs can start out with great ideas and intentions, building a company by doing things right and winning over their customers and employees. But once the money starts rolling in, they often forget about everything they stood for in the beginning. The employees who made them successful become secondary to their desire for a trendy, expensive car; instead of concentrating on providing great service to customers, they might raise prices so they can buy a bigger house or a boat. Success can make many people lose sight of the very priorities that made them successful in the first place. Their mission and purpose can move quickly from serving people to serving just one person: themselves. When that happens, it's a recipe for disaster and proof that a company has lost its vision. The leaders no longer understand that the business isn't there to serve them—it's there to provide jobs and stable careers, and a dream for your employees. The leader who says, "These people ought to be grateful that I give them a job" has got gratitude all wrong. Those leaders need to look inward, figure out what they're doing wrong, and find out the reasons why their employees don't love their jobs—it could very well be the leaders themselves.

FIVE WAYS TO BECOME A GRATEFUL LEADER

- Show gratitude to those who serve with you. It can be something as simple as saying "Thank you for everything you do" to your employees, and "Thanks for putting your trust in us" to your customers. Or you can come up with unique, creative ways to show your gratitude that has real value for those you serve.

- Inspire gratitude in others. Few people will ever find themselves in a position as unique as yours. You have a lot of responsibility, but ultimately your goal is to inspire, and particularly to inspire gratitude in others. Show them through your leadership that they, too, should be grateful and show gratitude to others. Being a leader means helping people, showing them the way, and giving them something that they don't have.

- Serve a higher purpose than yourself. Ultimately, people will believe in the higher purpose and the leaders who exemplify that purpose. If you want to build a business to serve yourself, you're going to have a difficult time convincing people to believe in that and want to do it. Build a business as a reflection of what's important to you. What do you stand for? How are you going to serve others? The answers to those questions are your higher purpose.

- Share what you learn. Teach what you know to those who are new to the trades. Pass your new knowledge on to your employees any way you can, whether it's through training, seminars, or even a company newsletter. Passing on your knowledge lifts everyone and serves your purpose and your people, and ultimately grows your company.

- Lead your customers and take care of them. Customers have many choices besides you and your company. If they've placed their trust in you, be grateful that they chose you to care for what's probably one of their more costly investments. Cherish and nurture those relationships. Always be the professional, and lead your customers in the right direction.

Chapter 3:

Create Your Vivid Vision

Today I had a new HVAC system installed in my condo. It was done by Peterman Heating, Cooling & Plumbing. The process began with a gentleman named Brandon who came out to do the estimate. When we decided to use Peterman for the project, a date was set for someone to come out and take measurements for a lift box for the furnace. John was the person who came to measure for that. The install had been scheduled for the next day, and two more gentlemen named Corey and Jose arrived on time to start the install process. The install was completed in one day, and my new system is working perfectly. I also had some contact with a lady named Lauren dealing with some last minute questions and issues. I cannot stress enough when saying that every person from Peterman was the ultimate professional. It seems that no matter what job or position they have within the company, they are very loyal to the company. Every question or issue that I had was answered or resolved quickly and to my total satisfaction. I'm sure I'm not the only one who has experienced this type of service from Peterman. Thanks to the company and all who had a hand in this transaction. You made it easy and memorable in a good way. Expect me to spread the word about your company and the service it provides. Thank you.

—Bob Smith, Noblesville, Indiana

I look forward to my morning routine because I give myself time to read. In fact, reading is the first thing I do when I awaken at 3:00 a.m. I'm awake before everyone else, the house is quiet, and I can read thoughtfully. I allow an hour for reading, and then I spend forty-five minutes afterward thinking about how to solve problems, and often the reading I just did helps me find solutions to those problems. I get some of my best ideas for improving the company from reading wonderful books written by business leaders, self-help experts, and others.

I read many books during my morning routine, and one book that has had a huge impact on me is *Vivid Vision: A Remarkable Tool for Aligning Your Business Around a Shared Vision of the Future*, by Cameron Herold. It's about detailing your vision for your company in a way that lets everyone in the company see what you, the entrepreneur, see in your mind for the future, and that vision becomes an important part of your company's culture. I read this book several years ago, and it hit home for me because we were turning a corner in our growth. Things were moving along very quickly, and we'd grown considerably. We in leadership had to think about bringing everyone together under our vision for the company's future and get our people's buy-in because we couldn't accomplish our goals by ourselves. We needed everyone's help and combined commitment to get there. Creating a Vivid Vision document played a large part in our successful growth.

Finding Our Vision

We had a vision, but it wasn't very detailed, and we didn't know how to express it to others. That's not uncommon—entrepreneurs often have a hard time sharing a vision with others. They start their own companies for many reasons, just like my dad did: being his own boss, making his own schedule, and doing something about which he was passionate. But business owners can become so caught up in the daily grind of solving problems and fixing issues that they often forget why they struck out on their own.

Sometimes, they start a company but don't think ahead to what their organization can become several years down the road. That's where I was at the time, with many questions bouncing around in my head about where we were going. Why are we growing? How are we growing? Is this going to take us to where we want to be even-

> But I came to understand that our company is all about people: how we can affect the lives of our employees and customers, and also how we can help improve our industry.

tually? *Vivid Vision* showed me that having a solid vision would answer all of these questions, and it guided me through defining our vision and sharing it.

To define the vision, I had to figure out whether our business serves a higher purpose, and that wasn't easy for me. I thought about what we do: we help customers with their residential heating and plumbing. That probably doesn't sound incredibly exciting to many people, and I wasn't sure what "higher purpose" means. But I came to understand that our company is all about people: how we can affect the lives of our employees and customers, and also how we can help improve our industry. My brother and I needed to explain this vision to our people in a way that they could understand it and relate it to themselves. We could have created a typical mission statement or vision statement and hope that everyone would rally to the cause. "Peterman is about people—our employees and their families, and our customers—and how we can affect their lives." But that statement (like most mission statements) isn't detailed enough, and more importantly, it doesn't tell employees what's in it for them. So getting everyone to buy into it would've been difficult. *Vivid Vision* was the answer. A Vivid Vision is different because it goes into great detail about what the future looks like and what it feels like to accomplish your goals. It involves everyone and makes it easy for them to see their individual roles in the company's success.

We approached our Vivid Vision from the perspective of improving and being successful while staying true to our higher purpose. We thought about several questions: Where are we going to take the company? How are we going to get better? How are we going to grow? How do we improve the lives of the people who work for us? The Vivid Vision answered these questions, as it helped us envision the future, and we weren't afraid to dream big while doing that. My brother and I learned to dream big at an early age because our parents always let us explore and try new things. They taught us to always think positively, which is important when creating a Vivid Vision. Both of us were involved in athletics from a very young age and were fortunate to play on some very good teams through high school and college. I don't think we ever went into a season doubting that we would win the championship. Did we always win it? No. But it was always our goal and part of our mindset that we could do whatever we believed we could do. That mindset has served my brother and me well in business, too, because we don't think that the industry standard of what a company should be is enough for us. We believe that we can do whatever we literally set our minds to, and the Vivid Vision has proven this out. Let's look at how to get started writing your own Vivid Vision.

Writing Your Vivid Vision

The author of *Vivid Vision* says that a Vivid Vision starts "when an entrepreneur, founder, or CEO plants one foot in the present and then leans out and places the other in the future, the 'what could be.'" Think a moment about what your company could be. Visualize what your company and people look like in the future, and then go even further and imagine what it feels like to be there when you accomplish your goals. This is how you create your Vivid Vision. You write about what you see in your future in great detail and then share it with everyone in your company.

Sharing your Vivid Vision is important for several reasons:

- You visualize your future success, which is inspiring for you and your people.
- You see your success in detail, which helps you align your actions toward success.
- Others are inspired to work toward success and to do so together.
- Others see a future for themselves and the company—together.
- Those who aren't inspired by it and don't see a future for themselves will likely leave, which is best for the company and all concerned.
- Sharing the vision empowers people to come up with ideas and solutions when faced with difficult situations.

The two key elements of creating the Vivid Vision are scripting and visualization.

Scripting and Visualization

Creating the Vivid Vision uses visualization techniques to imagine what the future looks like and scripting to write it out in the form of a document. Scripting is writing the story of your company's goals and future success based on how you want it to be. But the difference between goal setting and scripting for your Vivid Vision is that you write about your success as if it has already happened. Another difference that makes *Vivid Vision* unique is its emphasis on how you'll feel in the future when your company accomplishes its goals. I found this aspect particularly fascinating because you'll rarely find any form of business planning that includes feelings.

I admit that people give me some weird looks when I tell them about scripting. But visualizations and scripting have helped my mind grasp our goals and make them real—the power of writing something down solidifies it. I've been exposed to several teachings that say that we as humans are self-fulfilling prophecies, so scripting aligns with that thought, and I fully believe that scripting is self-fulfilling—that is, whatever it is that you believe you can do, writing it down will make it real, and you'll do it. But if you think you can't do something, then you probably won't be able to do it. If you plant an image, a goal, and a realization in your subconscious mind, your actions will follow it, and you'll start doing what you need to do to make your goals happen. It doesn't matter if you're having a tough day or are slow with work; you're still moving forward toward your goals. If you can tie your work today to your vision for the future in this way, I think your odds of success are far more favorable.

Scripting takes practice. Some people find it hard to think so positively and write about an uplifting, successful future as if it's already happened. But the more you practice, the easier it becomes to see and feel success and know you can reach it. At Peterman, we teach scripting to our people to use for their personal goal setting.

Steps to Writing the Vivid Vision

To get started creating your Vivid Vision, pick a time three years in the future. (I personally like a three-year time frame. It's easy for me to envision because it isn't too far in the future.) You might use your company fiscal year date to start. Pretend you're walking through your company's facility and are going to write about everything you see, hear, and feel on that day three years in the future. Walk through every department in the company, every room in every building, and even walk into your customers' facilities (or homes if your business serves people at home, as ours does) to envision all aspects of your company in operation as you want them to be three years from now.

- What do you see and hear?
- What are your employees doing?
- What are they talking about?
- How is each department running?
  Is it organized and efficient?
- How are your customers doing?
- What are your customers saying about you?
- What does your community think about you?
- What do your marketing efforts look like?
  How are they working?

- Do you offer any new products or services?
- In what areas is the company focused?
- In what areas are you personally focused?
- What does your company culture look like? Are employees living your core values?
- How are the company finances?
- How are you interacting with your stakeholders?
- Has the company increased its reach?
- How do you feel about what you see?
  How do your employees feel?

Take notes about what you see during this exercise, and use them to write a detailed description of what you saw in the future for each department in the company. Write only what you saw and felt, not how anything you saw came to be. That's one of the interesting things about Vivid Vision—you see the future, but you don't know how you got there, and you don't write anything at all about how these things were accomplished (I'll discuss more on this later). The resulting document is your company's Vivid Vision.

Peterman's Vivid Vision

My brother and I wrote our Vivid Vision document at the end of 2016, a seven-page document that sketches out what we wanted the company to look like in three years. Our Vivid Vision described every department in the company in detail as we saw it in three years— what kind of people work there, how they think and feel, what they accomplish, what we'll be known for at that time, who our customers will be and what they think of us, how we'll communicate, what our culture will look like, and so on. The document is written as if it's already three years later, in the present tense. Here's an example from our document:

PARTS DEPARTMENT

Our growing parts department is continuing to keep material costs down and inventory levels accurate. Our parts department and warehouse team are extremely efficient and utilize ServiceTitan to run it extremely efficiently. Both plumbing service and HVAC service technicians utilize the parts department to stay efficient out in the field. Our parts department handles all the warranty claims and helps continually update price books. We continue to find ways in this department to increase efficiency in the company.

This section is a great example because I recently learned that our inventory levels have improved dramatically since we wrote that about a year and a half ago because of some new processes we put in place that align with this Vivid Vision statement. So it took much less time to accomplish that goal than we expected when we wrote the statement. That's how it works sometimes with Vivid Vision— things might happen quickly or take more time, but they do happen.

We knew how we wanted people to operate and interact within the business, but I think our ideas and goals took on a lot more power once we wrote them out in our document. At first, we had no idea what would happen when we started writing the document—we just wrote it by following the guidance in the book, crossing our fingers, and sharing it with our people. It was amazing how everyone related to our Vivid Vision and became excited about our goals and their roles in reaching them. Because of the details in the document, their roles were clear to them, and they now had a vision for their own success. This experience has made us huge believers in this method of creating a vision and realizing it. Many of the books that I've read—whether it's Lee Milteer's *Success Is an Inside Job: The Secrets to Getting Anything You Want* or Maxwell Maltz's *Psycho Cybernetics*—discuss planting images and goals in your subconscious mind of where you want to be and how your conscious mind will chase after those goals, often without you knowing it. We took a leap of faith in using these teachings to realize our goals and really strive for them, but for us, it truly worked. When we first wrote our visions and goals in this way, we were a bit skeptical and thought, "Wow, it's going to take a lot of effort to get to these goals!" But here's a fact: we accomplished about 90 percent of the goals in that document within the first year—not the three years we'd planned for in the document, but in the first year! There was no greater proof in my mind that if we planted this vision in the subconscious, we would get there. When we accomplished goals in the document, we revised it with more goals, often setting a higher bar to reach because we felt that confident in our method.

You can also use this technique with individual departments. We asked each manager to script out what their department would look like after the first quarter, and they refer to that document to understand what they're working toward and how it all fits into the bigger picture of the company's Vivid Vision. The department-level document and the company's Vivid Vision also delivered another benefit: accountability. Everyone wanted to reach these goals, and no one wanted to be sitting there three years later wondering why we didn't accomplish some or all of them. Mostly, I think it allowed us to dream bigger and set higher goals in the document revision. We accomplished a lot in one year, so why not raise that bar up a bit higher?

We found the Vivid Vision process really was as easy as putting it down on paper and saying, "I think we can do this—I *know* we can do this!"

Share the Vision

Creating a Vivid Vision makes the difficult task of sharing your vision with employees much easier, particularly in showing them their part in your future success. An employee who isn't in a leadership role in a business is generally going to work only within their capacity if that's all you give them. But creating a shared vision gives them something much bigger to strive for, something incredible that can be accomplished if everyone goes for it together. When you tie their role in the company to something bigger than they are, it generates a lot of excitement, and you'll see plenty of progress because everyone's rowing the boat in the same direction. Without a vision of what the company will look like in the future, that person can't have a vision of their own career and success, either, because they can't be sure what the coming years might bring for them. Maybe the owner wants to sell the company or stop it from getting any bigger—it could be any number of things that directly affect that employee. But the shared vision keeps employees from having to guess what the owner wants, and they'll know whether the company vision aligns with their personal vision. We saw this firsthand in the excitement our Vivid Vision generated among our people and their drive to have a part in fulfilling our positive vision for the future.

Accomplishing the Vivid Vision

The process of creating a Vivid Vision is to write only about what you see, but not how you accomplished it all. I found that quite interesting. We didn't have an implementation plan—we just went day by day and let it happen. That probably surprises you, and I was a bit skeptical at first. We read the document multiple times throughout the year—at company meetings, for example. But we didn't have a step-by-step process for achieving those goals. I think that just writing those ideas down aligned our actions to what we wanted to do. We didn't consciously say, "Hey, we wrote this in a Vivid Vision; we might want to get started doing this." A Vivid Vision creates the mindset and environment for achievement, and we found ourselves reading the document throughout the year and being surprised that we'd accomplished many of the things we'd written without being aware of it. I think the fact that we know where we're going and we continue to get there inspires our people. They know we're creating something bigger than just making money for the owner, and that automatically aligns our actions in the correct way.

Here's an example of something I believe we accomplished because our Vivid Vision gave all of us a growth mindset and drove us toward the bigger picture. We wrote in our document, "We have an HR manager and full-time recruiter." We didn't have either of those when we wrote the document, but we hired one about nine months later. Although having an HR manager was a goal, ultimately the bigger picture was that we were going to continue growing overall as a company and want to keep growing. That continual growth led us to hire the HR manager and eventually a full-time recruiter because we had grown so much that we needed them.

- To make your Vivid Vision successful, keep these four key points in mind:
- Understand what you want. You as the entrepreneur know what you ultimately want your company to be. You started it and you run it, so you need to decide what you want out of it. For us, our Vivid Vision is to make this the best place our people have ever worked and to change our industry. Not every heating and plumbing company out there wants to change the industry or really cares about making it the best place any of their people ever worked. But we believe that if we aim for those two things, we're going to provide the best customer service to our customers, and we're going to grow our people, who then take care of our customers.
- Write those things down as your Vivid Vision. Follow the steps to writing the Vivid Vision. Use your imagination, and take time to feel what it will feel like in the future when you accomplish those goals because you want to feel something different, and that's what creating something bigger is about. You have to feel it because ultimately that's what guides your actions. Day in and day out, you must have that feeling of where you want to end up.
- Understand what it's going to take to get to your goals, and be willing to do what it takes. It's easy to write something big down on paper, that rosy-red picture of what your company's going to look like, but you also have to work hard to make it happen, and you have to be willing to do that hard work. If you aren't, the Vivid Vision won't ever come to fruition. Some people have said that Vivid Vision is like magic—and it is to

a certain degree—but again, it's hard work, and my brother and I aren't afraid of it. Sometimes I'd work until three o'clock every morning. I'm sure some people would think that's crazy, and there were days when I wondered about that myself.

- Be genuine about your Vivid Vision, and inspire people to the vision. It can't be lip service because people will see right through that, and you're going to have to live the document once you write it. If all you really care about is putting money into your pocket and that's what you write as your Vivid Vision, you won't have many people who want to work for you. You have to connect that vision to what's in it for everyone (and make sure there *is* something in it for everyone). Inspire them to want something greater, to want to put in the extra work, and to want to better themselves for the betterment of the company. If you can get them to do that and understand that there's a future for them, they'll start doing things in the best interest of the company. You can't do this alone; you need other people and their buy-in.

When you can connect those four points, your gas tank never runs out. Your Vivid Vision becomes part of you, and when it does, you can inspire others to believe in it, and that's when the magic happens. That's when you can truly reach goals that others thought were impossible. But all four elements have to be connected. If one of them is out of whack, you won't accomplish what you want. Suppose you do a great job of writing down what you want; you paint the picture, feel all the feelings, and understand it all, but you're not willing to put in the work. That's a disconnect, and you're never going to get to your goals. The magic won't happen. When it all connects, you generate momentum and start to fulfill that Vivid Vision.

Vivid Vision Results

Your Vivid Vision is a living document, meaning you can add to it and make changes. It doesn't have to stay exactly the way you wrote it at the start. This is particularly true if you find yourself accomplishing goals faster than you expected. You can add new goals, which is what we did when we started reaching our initial goals in fewer than three years. But we keep our document time frame at three years to reach goals, mostly because I find it easier to see three years ahead. Many companies make five- or ten-year plans, but I think a three-year time frame creates a sense of urgency, just enough to stop you from putting things off and risking not accomplishing them. One of the hallmarks of our company is that we move quickly. If we need to make changes to improve a process or how we provide service, for example, we'll make those changes right away. It's good for the business too. As our world moves faster, our people are more excited about the company and their place in it, and they're more anxious to see progress. So a three-year plan makes good sense for many reasons.

A company that has a Vivid Vision plan for the future is never caught saying, "What are we doing today?" Many companies never look past tomorrow, but with a Vivid Vision in place, you always know what you're doing and why you're doing it. Without a plan in general, let alone a vision, employees will lose interest quickly because they're not working toward something bigger than they are. To get people to give you and your company their best career years, you must provide them with a detailed, inspiring vision for them that looks into the future. They have to be excited about what's going on in the company, and they have to want to better themselves.

Since we put our Vivid Vision in place at Peterman, we're on pace to grow by more than 30 percent again for the third year in a row. I don't think that's a coincidence. The Vivid Vision sets the tone for our organization, clearly defining what we're all about and what we're going to do. It also details how we're going to grow and what it looks and feels like when we reach those goals.

> To get people to give you and your company their best career years, you must provide them with a detailed, inspiring vision for them that looks into the future.

Write your own Vivid Vision. Take time to get away from the office and dream about what you first set out to do when you started your company. Do you still have all the energy and gusto that you had when you first started out and thought you had a great idea, or are you just tearing through each day just to get through it? If you've lost that initial energy and enthusiasm, you can find it again through the Vivid Vision. I'm not guaranteeing you'll have it every day. I go through some tough days now and then and find myself thinking, "I just need to get through today." But ultimately, I can sit back, look at the Vivid Vision, and realize two things that are extremely important to me as a business owner and leader: a lot of people are counting on me, and this is what I said we were going to do—and we're going to do it together as a team.

Chapter 4:

Empower Your People to Dream Big

Our air conditioner stopped working on a ninety-degree day, so we reached out to Peterman mainly due to the high reviews. I am so glad we did! Our technician was Dave, and he was not only extraordinary at his job, but he's an honest and genuine individual as well. He was very thorough and skilled at making the repair. He made a difficult, potentially extremely expensive, situation a pleasure. He only fixed the source of the problem rather than attempting to upsell in any way. Thank you so much for getting us up and running again so quickly.

—Jennifer B.

Peterman's strong company culture focused on people is the core of our business success. While other companies might operate based on business first and people second, we at Peterman know that our most valuable resource is our people. Without them, we wouldn't be growing and successful like we are today. But within our people-focused culture lies the *real* secret to our success: empowering people. We empower our people to do their best and be their best, and in doing so, amazing things have happened for both our company and our people.

What does it mean to empower someone? Empowerment is leadership giving people the power to do their best and be their best so they can become stronger and more confident; thus they affect your business in positive ways. It's showing trust in them by giving them the freedom to do their best and do the right thing for themselves and the company. My greatest teachers were the people who empowered me to be my best, and I learned from them that empowering people is an important part of leadership. Empowering employees has many benefits for a company because empowered people will do the following:

- Be more productive
- Go the extra mile beyond what's expected of them
- Follow best practices
- Communicate better with each other, with leadership, and with your customers
- Embrace change because they don't fear it
- Have a positive attitude and a mindset for dreaming big
- Provide better customer service
- Be loyal to you and your company
- Work better with each other
- Spread the good word about your company as a wonderful place to work
- Enjoy better lives away from work because they're happy and less stressed

Empowerment and Trust

It takes time to build an empowering infrastructure in a company, mostly because leadership can be hesitant to give people more autonomy, which some view as giving up control. To empower people, you have to show that you trust them. Empowered people are more apt to follow you than they would if you're a dictator who tells them what to do and how they should do their jobs. Dictating to people won't connect you with them in meaningful ways, and it keeps them from doing their best because they must do everything your way—even if their way might be better than yours might. Leaders and managers are responsible for creating the systems within which people can be great. I know I'm a better leader whenever I can give people freedom and opportunities, both of which have been crucial to our company's growth. I know that our company won't grow if we don't give people the resources they need to be their best. The company

> We empower our people to do their best and be their best, and in doing so, amazing things have happened for both our company and our people.

would stop growing, and no one would see me as a great leader. I believe that if I can make everyone feel empowered to do their jobs to the best of their ability and figure things out for themselves, we'll always grow.

I come right out and tell people that I trust them. Any time we're trying to solve a problem, I'll say, "Whatever you think is right. I trust you. We're all in this together. If you think that's what's right for the customer, make the decision. Let's do it." If you don't trust anybody to make a decision except yourself, then you're going to struggle to grow. I think you see this in many small businesses. The owner wants to make every decision on the face of the earth and be involved in every discussion. They can't ever grow because no one in their organization feels like they can make a decision, and they always have to check in with the owner. With trust comes empowerment because once people realize that you trust them, they'll make their own decisions based on their expertise and will likely make some decisions that are better than yours might have been. I think trust unlocks a lot of growth potential within an organization.

Our company is growing so quickly, but it's not me doing the growing. All of our people feel empowered to grow, and I'm just a piece in the puzzle. Nothing makes me happier than talking with someone who tells me they've solved a big problem or figured out a process on their own. I know that I've empowered that person to take responsibility and initiative and provided them with the resources they need to be great. Doing this creates a culture in which people are just running every day—running to get better, to do more, and to do everything they can to continually improve. When businesses can create an environment like that, people are attracted to it and will do more than just what's asked of them.

People take great satisfaction in reaching a goal or doing something that no one thought was possible. Accomplishing work, growing, and feeling empowered to be better than you were yesterday is addicting for those who want to continue to improve. But it's not addicting for those who like the status quo and are fearful of change. Such people tend to see problems in everything, feel stress daily, and are afraid to grow. Empowered people don't think that way. They're not afraid to dream big and try new things, to take initiative and come up with ideas to make processes work better. We're game to let them try new things and will always give it a shot.

> Doing this creates a culture in which people are just running every day—running to get better, to do more, and to do everything they can to continually improve.

The worst we can do is say, "Well, that didn't work," and start all over again.

Empowerment Benefits Everyone

Empowering others has made me less stressed when leading more than 120 employees than I was when we had only twenty-two people in the company (and I was employee number 22 when I started). Others find that hard to believe, but I feel less stressed simply because we've hired so many great people and empowered them to do great things. The only stress I have is from wondering whether I'm providing them with enough resources to keep them going at the pace they want to improve themselves. I don't ever want to stunt anybody's growth.

Our culture encourages everyone to empower each other. No matter what position you're in, can you empower somebody? We train our department heads to empower everyone who works for them directly. A lead installer should empower his or her apprentice; someone in the office who's been here a while should empower a new employee. I like to say that empowering others will ultimately get you more. Think about it. If you're in customer service and you empower others by teaching them your processes and procedures, they'll do a great job, which can lead to us hiring more people and creating a better position for you. Our goal is to provide the best place to work—I can't say that often enough. The best place to work is one in which you literally feel as if there are no bounds on you whatsoever. It's when people think, "How good can I get? Where can I go? I know I can do it."

I love it when everyone has the mindset of empowering others. I've always wanted Peterman to be a company that we all build together because there will always be a place for everybody.

Empowering Others to Dream Big

Our culture revolves around giving people tools to be successful. Empowering people to dream big is giving them a special tool—a mindset to think big. We help them understand that they can achieve anything they set out to do. One way we do this is through our Future Leaders program, most of which is mindset based. We help our people to articulate their dreams and plant them in their minds as personal Vivid Visions of their own careers and dreams. I often find that people don't shoot high enough when thinking about their futures. For example, they might think about moving up one level in their jobs, but what happens once that's accomplished? Where are you going next? Dreaming big means moving past the internal barriers that keep you from moving forward and tell you that can't do something. Dreaming big means believing you can do anything you want to do.

Success comes from the actions you take daily to achieve goals, so we help our people learn how to work toward their goals. For example, someone says, "I want to make this amount of money." So how are they going to achieve that goal? Often, they're not sure. So we dig deeper and ask what actions they could take today that would move them closer to that goal—what could they do with their customers, which questions they could ask, and the extra steps they could take to bring them closer to their goal. This process of questioning is something people don't often do. We show them that the little things are ultimately going to take them to their big dream and they have complete control over their life outcomes. This is a big aspect of helping people to grow because it's hard to dream big if you think you can't control the outcome. When they believe they're in control, we see different actions develop that help them and propel the company forward. This is personal career coaching, though people can use these principles to achieve goals in their personal lives too.

When empowering people to dream big, we emphasize the following points to help them be successful:

- Don't be afraid to dream. Society tells us that if you dream big, you're probably going to be disappointed. Remember that you have complete control of your goals, so no matter how big the dream, you have the power to achieve it.

- Believe that the dream will come true. Belief is what keeps you moving toward the dream. If you have doubts, you might hesitate to take the actions necessary to realize your dream.

- Visualize your dream, and be very specific. You have to be specific to know exactly what you're trying to achieve.

- Set some checkpoints that you can measure. This is how you'll know you're making progress (or not).

- Align those checkpoints with your daily actions. The actions you take should lead you to the next checkpoint of progress.

- Stay focused. This is where visualizing the goal is critical. If you're not focused and passionate about the goal, it's difficult to reach it.

- Avoid excuses. That's the easy way out. Instead of thinking, "I can't do that because … " try thinking, "I *can* do that because … " You'll likely find many more reasons why you can achieve a dream than you'll find excuses for not achieving it.

- Don't be afraid to fail. If at first you don't succeed, try, try again. It's an old adage, but it's true, and we live that at Peterman. We're not afraid to fail. Even if you come up short at a checkpoint, you'll be a lot closer to your goal than you would be if you hadn't done anything at all.

- Go easy on yourself during tough times. Don't be too hard on yourself if you fail or have setbacks. You can't hit the ball out of the park every time at bat. Just keep moving forward toward the dream.

- Take care of yourself. Don't push yourself so hard that you can't accomplish anything. You have to be at your best when striving to achieve your goals.

Dreaming Big: True Stories

A technician with an apartment maintenance background, Joey answered one of our online job ads, and we scheduled an interview with him. I admit that when our service manager and I set up the interview, we didn't have the highest hopes in the world for a good outcome. The people we've encountered with apartment maintenance backgrounds know a little bit about a lot of things, but—this is critical for us—they haven't really dealt much with customers. In apartment maintenance, technicians fix problems as called upon, and normally, they're in the apartment by themselves. If they do encounter the renter, they aren't really doing serious customer service functions because the renter doesn't own their home, and they're not buying anything. Even though the technician knows how to fix the problems, they typically have zero customer interface experience.

Joey showed us that had some technical knowledge, but he told us, "I don't know everything, but I've seen a lot of different technical situations and have taken on some different roles." What we noticed most about him in the interview was that he was quite genuine. He was just a good guy who we could tell was definitely motivated, definitely hungry, and very confident, which is great. When we asked him, "Where do you see yourself in five years?" he said to the service manager, "I'd like to be in your spot." His attitude was a huge plus in our minds, and we certainly didn't tell him that was impossible. We said, "By all means, we want to take you on that journey." Despite his lack of certain experiences, we knew we could work with him, and we really needed someone, so we hired him.

Sure enough, Joey jumped right in and started learning from the service manager and the other technicians. He didn't disappoint us. From the time he started, I always kept an eye on him because he was hungry to improve. Any time we gave him a task, he would not only do the job, but also give us great ideas on how to do things better.

Eventually, when we wanted to start our home performance division in the company last year, Joey was the first person we tapped to be in charge of leading this new division, and he definitely ran with it. He's responsible for getting the crew going and making in-home visits to talk with homeowners about how their homes can be more efficient. As he got that position up and running, we also had him helping out in our excavation department, where we were a bit light on people. We asked him to help that department because he's so passionate, versatile, and skilled. So he's running his own division and helping in another. Most people who take on so much extra responsibility would be tired, but he comes in with more energy every day and is ready to help in any way he can. The only negative thing I ever hear from him is, "I think I can do more; I think I'm not doing enough. I think I can do more."

One of the reasons I think Joey is so successful is because he's so genuine and loves this company. He eats, sleeps, and breathes what he is providing. Now, we had to find the right person, and most of his success is directly attributable to him. But we also gave him a platform from which he feels that he can be as successful as he ultimately wants to be. He doesn't see any barriers to his success, and his career can go wherever he wants it to take him. I get most excited when I see the fire in somebody and we can give that person what he or she needs to use it. If we didn't give Joey that, I don't think he'd have that fire and confidence in himself. Many times, it's himself that he's selling to the customer or presenting in a service matter. His confidence was his platform for dreaming, and that's what empowerment means. When we empower our people, we give them confidence that they can break the mold, break out of the stereotypes, and dream big, and we give them a platform to accomplish those dreams. Joey is a true testament to what we're trying to do at Peterman and the platform that we want to build for our people here.

> When we empower our people, we give them confidence that they can break the mold, break out of the stereotypes, and dream big, and we give them a platform to accomplish those dreams.

Our growth has taught our people that they don't have to stay in the same position for their entire careers. They've seen some of their peers who were service technicians or installers move up into different roles in the company, take on management responsibility, or move to different departments and take on other responsibilities. They're seeing these people dream big and have career goals and aspirations that they're achieving, which I think is critical, especially in an industry that typically doesn't give people opportunities to improve and grow. We give them those opportunities to be more than they ever dreamed they could be.

Another lesson from this story is about our service manager's reaction to the technician saying he wanted his job. People are often naturally inclined to hold someone back because they're afraid the person will grow and surpass them. But the service manager didn't do that and, in fact, did everything he could to help the technician succeed. He empowered his new employee to be his best and was a great example of putting Peterman's culture and values into action.

Peterman's employees have the same fire to improve and make things better. Ultimately, when you have many such people, growth isn't so challenging or daunting because everyone is growing in the same direction toward making the company a better place. We'll go to great lengths to hire people who have that fire. In fact, we once hired someone even though we didn't have an open position for her.

We received a résumé from a woman who had run her own company like ours for twenty years. She was well known within our business community because her father had started their company, and like me, she eventually ran it. I was immediately intrigued when I saw her résumé, and all I could think was, "How do I get her on our team? How do I get someone with the knowledge, skills, and the understanding of our industry that she has, even though we don't have a role for her?" I remembered hearing that her father had passed away and the family sold the company, so that explained why her résumé was now crossing my desk. But I wasn't interested in just her experience in our industry. I got that feeling again that I get when I see someone who I know would be a perfect fit at Peterman. I look at many résumés and always through the lens of getting the right people on our team, people I know can make an impact and we can affect. Despite not having a position for her, I called her in for an interview.

She had wanted to do many of the things we were doing at her own company, but she never got the chance. I knew that we could make an impact on her and show her that it's possible to do things differently from how our industry usually operates, and that we make many happy customers that way. She was impressed with how we could change the way things are done on a big scale, take care of many people, and provide customer service at a very high level at the same time. She wanted to be part of it all, and I knew we could use her skills, so we offered her a position as our customer assurance specialist, and we ended up making a good team. In this case, the company dreamed big. The fact that we didn't have an open position didn't stop us from hiring someone who we knew would fit in, make a difference, and be part of our Vivid Vision. Dreaming big works both ways.

Overcoming Negative Attitudes Through Empowerment

Empowered people can overcome many negative things in their lives. We use empowerment to help our people overcome the negative attitudes and stereotypes people have of our industry, particularly toward tradespeople. Society has a general outlook that everyone should go to college. Not everyone chooses to go, sometimes because they don't think it's right for them. Others can't afford to go and can't find financial options to make it happen. Many of those people go into the trades, and there's a lot of pride in being skilled in a trade that I think is overshadowed by the notion that everyone should go to college. The trades aren't necessarily the most glamorous jobs, but that doesn't mean that tradespeople shouldn't be proud of their work and what they do.

Attitudes born of the go-to-college mindset can often affect how people deal with tradespeople ("contractors"). Long-held stereotypes and bad experiences with contractors also contribute to people's negative attitudes. They're sometimes afraid a contractor will take advantage of them or not complete the work to the customer's satisfaction. I've heard many negative things that people say about contractors. "They never called me back. They didn't show up on time. He looks really grungy and dirty. He's going to trounce through my house and make a mess. They never do what they said they're going to do. There's always an upcharge at the end. They're trying to sell me a bill of goods or say something's broken when it isn't." I've even heard people say, "Can I trust this guy in my home if my wife was there alone? Can I trust him with my kids in the house?" In our business, this is very disheartening.

Part of our mission at Peterman is to change these attitudes and people's outlook on having work done in their homes so that they no longer fear it. We want them to look at tradespeople as professionals and understand that as long as you vet the company properly, you shouldn't be concerned about the work because professionals will take care of you. But to do that, we have to address all of these stereotypes directly with our own people first because it is so disheartening when others view you and your industry with such negativity collectively. They know about people's preconceived notions—all of that chatter is in their heads—and they often feel powerless to do anything about it. We've found that our empowerment culture helps them overcome the stereotypes and actually change customers' attitudes. As we empower our people to dream big, we have to face all of the negative attitudes head-on, come up with ways to counteract the thinking, and empower our people to form their own, positive ways to change how customers think about our industry.

We ask our people, "What will make you different? What will make you stand out? What will make customers change their minds and attitudes about those in our industry?" The upside to winning customers' hearts and minds is that we don't have a huge hill to climb—the industry already has a low reputation. If our people are courteous to the customer and make sure that they complete the work as we expect them to do, they're going to be far better than most contractors are. Empowerment in this case is emphasizing that they should expect more from themselves. They shouldn't include them-selves in that group of stereotypical contractors. We empower them to be different from—and better than—the norm in our industry. Our job is to get the technicians to get out of their own way because they've placed themselves in a box of, "Well, this is what I do. This is all I can ever do. I'm always going to be this."

Showing genuine interest and great caring is at the heart of changing attitudes and empowering our people to change them. The stereotypes are stereotypes for a reason, most likely because people's repeated negative experiences with those in our industry proved them out. I'd like to say that what people think about contractors is baseless, but I can't because the negative experiences have surely happened. I've emphasized to our people that dispelling stereotypes is part of their jobs as professionals. Our people make sure our customers know that we don't act that way, and our company doesn't operate like that. Our goal is to provide an experience such as the customer would find in a fine restaurant or a high-end department store. We take extra steps in providing service that make customers feel special. For example, we offer Chore of Your Choice for customers who are members of our Peterman Protection Club (our service agreements), and I'm pretty sure that other companies don't do this. If a customer has a small chore that needs done—hanging a picture on the wall, changing a light bulb, or changing batteries in a smoke detector, for example—our guys will take care of it. They're already at your home. Many customers who take advantage of this benefit are elderly. Chore of the Day is beyond the norm and goes a long way toward changing customers' attitudes, even the most ingrained stereotypes. Just as important, it empowers our people to effect changes by being their best and doing their best.

Any business can come up with extra services that will make customers sit up and take notice. Other service extras we provide that most companies like ours don't include the following:

- Checking in with the customer on the day of their service
- Sending out a picture of the technician who's coming to their home, along with a short biography
- Calling the customer after the job to follow up and make sure everything was okay with the service call (known as a "happy call")
- Always wearing booties in the customer's home to show that we care about their property
- Treating our customers' homes as if they were our own

Providing such extras and the training we give our people in customer service is against the stereotypical image and part of how we dream big as a company. We might not change the entire industry overnight, but we've seen the difference in customers' attitudes and, most importantly, in our own people's self-confidence.

Create a Culture of Empowerment

Deciding to create a culture of empowerment in your company could be the most empowering thing you do for yourself as a leader. The mutual trust that comes from empowerment reaffirms that you believe in your people and in yourself as their leader. I firmly believe that everyone wins when you commit to empowering people, and as you know by now, we're all about winning at Peterman. From our experience, here are eight tactics you can use to empower people to be their best:

1. **Help people create their personal Vivid Visions.**
    Many people don't have a vision for their career or job. We share Peterman's Vivid Vision with our people so they can see their roles in our success, and we guide their personal success by creating their personal Vivid Vision using the same processes described in chapter 3 for a company Vivid Vision. It's their first step in dreaming big.

2. **Give them a path of growth.**
    A job is a dead end in many companies in our industry. Peterman is different because we make growth paths for our employees, and it's one of our best retention practices. People are happier and more productive when they know a company cares enough about them to give them a real future.

3. **Live the behaviors that you want them to embrace.**
    Being a dictator won't motivate people, and telling others what to do is the least effective way to get them to change. The best way is to be an example and a model of behavior

by living the behaviors, actions, and values we want to see in them. This requires commitment and discipline from me as the leader, and I know that I have to be the person I want my team to be.

4. **Give them the power to do things on their own.**

   I don't micromanage and never will because that's another way to completely kill motivation. I give people space to figure things out, and I've seen how it increases their motivation. Many business owners probably think it's scary to give people more freedom, but my experience shows that it's not scary, but rather the most powerful thing you can do. Our people have proven it in their performance and results, which are better than I could have imagined.

5. **Let your people find solutions.**

   I don't give everyone the answers to problems; rather I let them find the answers themselves. This is less about managing them than it is about managing myself. It's easy to just give people the answers, but if you do that, they'll never learn. They need to try and even fail if they're going to learn and grow. Do you automatically give everyone the answers when a problem arises, or do you let people find their own solutions?

6. **Be a giver.**

   Giving to people empowers them. It doesn't have to be material things. Give them your time, your trust, your knowledge, and your belief in them. This can mean far more to them than any material gift because giving them these things empowers and inspires them.

7. **Forgive their mistakes.**

   As a company, we've made many mistakes as we've grown. But we view mistakes as teaching and learning moments, so if our people make mistakes, we know they'll become better from the experience. It doesn't do anyone any good to get angry about mistakes. Forgive those who make mistakes, and help them find the lessons in the experiences.

8. **Praise their efforts.**

This goes hand in hand with forgiving mistakes. Even if people make mistakes, at least they're trying. Praising those efforts encourages them to learn and grow.

Chapter 5:

The Cadence of Culture

Peterman's was a wonderful company to do business with from start to finish! They were attentive, competent, and thorough with a very challenging job. I felt confident about every step. They even cleaned up with extra care! I will now be using them for other services, too, like plumbing. I was very impressed.

—Catherine C.

You created a winning culture for your company, and your people are embracing it, but how do you maintain it and keep it going? Your culture must have a cadence or rhythm—an ongoing, regular beat—and it's constant, 24/7, 365 days a year. The cadence of a company culture means constantly living, working, and reinforcing your company values and goals through the things you do for your employees regularly. I described some of the programs and benefits that Peterman offers employees, and that's a big part of our culture. But beyond programs and benefits, companies need to do much more to keep that rhythm going.

I've seen many companies struggle with maintaining the cadence of their culture. I think a big mistake they often make is thinking they can fix a culture problem by trying to do some of the fun things they read about that bigger companies do, especially Silicon Valley tech companies. Those companies have plenty of money and resources to invest in extravagant perks (like gaming rooms, ping-pong tables, and the like), but these types of things don't really affect culture. A company can provide plenty of perks, but culture goes much deeper and is based on values and mission. It takes hard work and effort to build a culture and even more hard work and effort to maintain it and keep the cadence going. Leaders must understand that sustaining a company culture must be one of their top priorities, or the culture and its benefits will fall flat. You need to reinforce your culture's focus (whatever it is) every hour of every day.

For example, if your culture centers on caring about your people, you have to think about it as a relationship. Frankly, it *is* a relationship, one between your company and its leaders and your people. At Peterman, we believe that a business is its people. We all know that relationships take work to maintain, but we have a relationship with each person who works here. We go out of our way to acknowledge people and pay attention to what's going on personally with each individual, and it's not just lip service—it's sincere interest. Just like a relationship, you have to be there for people and show them that you care.

I knew that our people would continue to grow and keep our culture growing, but still I had concerns about how to maintain the wonderful, positive momentum our culture was experiencing. We tried many different things and found several strategies that have been successful for us in keeping our cadence of culture beating strongly:

- Constantly reinforce your culture.
- Recognize your people's successes.
- Keep your door open.
- Constantly hire for your culture.
- Keep your finger on the pulse of your company.

I'll discuss the importance of each of these strategies in this chapter. Together, they keep us focused on our core values, mission, and beliefs and strengthen our culture every day.

Constantly Reinforce Your Culture

We keep our cadence of our culture going by making culture part of everything we do. Any time we communicate with employees— for example, through emails, our training sessions, coaching, and company events—it is an opportunity to reinforce our company culture and core values and to make sure that everyone knows their role in helping our company to thrive. Our all-company meeting held on the first Monday of the month is a good example of how we live our culture together as a team.

Company meetings are important to reinforcing the sense of being a team and showing that each person matters, and any company can use its all-hands meetings to its advantage. But leaders must plan these meetings well, or they can have the opposite effect. You don't want people to dread coming to meetings, so you have to create an agenda that will hold everyone's attention and make each employee feel that they spent their time well. Most companies use meetings to commu-nicate new information to their people, and we do that, too, but we don't have earth-shattering news to share every time. Our strategy for creating a winning agenda is to have fun and build camaraderie, so we include cultural items in each meeting. Many business owners might think that fun, team-building meetings would be the least productive kind to have, but we've found that they're the most productive. Any time you gather your entire team together is a don't-miss opportunity to engage people and keep the cadence of culture going.

A typical Peterman company meeting opens with me welcoming everyone, and then I ask people to state one thing for which they're grateful. I think this gets us all in the right frame of mind before moving on with the agenda. People can mention anything that they're grateful for, and it doesn't have to be about work, but often it is. For example, our marketing manager said in a meeting, "I'm grateful for this place where I work. Last week when I was away, I missed all of the people who work with me." Hearing this not only tells me that I'm doing my job, but it's great for our team to know that others care about them and enjoy working with them, and it shows them what a special place this is to work. After this, we introduce any new people who have joined our team.

I like to spend time talking about our Vivid Vision and share any updates we've made to it. I also discuss our core values and our mission and how we're going to accomplish it. Our employees all carry a wallet card that divides our game plan for reaching our goals and operating as a company into four sections: family growth, higher-purpose service, service to significance, and "know to grow." These are our most important priorities if we're going to reach our goals, and reviewing them during meetings reinforces those values we teach. I talk a little bit about every point on the card and ask questions to get the team's input.

This is just one example of a culture focus in a company meeting. It makes the meeting interesting and holds your team's attention because you can interact with them and have discussions. Planning great meetings takes a lot of time and effort, but it's worth it because employees look forward to attending them, and everyone leaves feeling stronger as a team. Our meetings are important and informative for everyone, especially as we continue to hire more people. But more importantly, they're a big part of the cadence of our culture, the rhythm that keeps it strong and growing. I organize the entire event, and it's so popular that we have nearly 100 percent attendance. We now have to rent an outside location for the meeting.

Win Today

Our culture is one of understanding what we need to do today to win today for the company and for our people. "Win today" is another strategy that reinforces our culture. We measure what winning means in many ways—for example, the number of successful installs we do in a week or a month, or team members competing for the most five-star customer reviews. We keep score on various metrics using a big whiteboard outside our call center, kind of like a scoreboard to post the metrics we measure from the previous day versus the current day. It keeps the cadence going in the office. We've found that if our office staff is enthusiastic and locked in to the mission, they encourage our people in the field, and we all do better. Everyone knows exactly what we need to do today to win and how to do it. But if we don't hit our goals, we don't get upset or look for someone to blame. Instead, we focus on the adjustments we need to make to get the win the next day.

We're going to shoot for goals, but ultimately, we have to enjoy the journey, even the rough spots on the road.

Winning today means the customer wins too. The people at Peterman go into more than one hundred homes a day, but they need to treat each customer as number one. We teach them to be in the present and focused on the call they're on, not to be thinking about the next call or the one after that. I want everyone on that call to consider that one customer their only priority for the day. If they have to stay there all day to take care of that customer, then that's what they'll do, and we'll figure out how to handle the rest of the calls for the day. Any time we can get everyone to be in the present like that, it's almost magical because customers just rave about the service. They truly feel as if our technician's only job that day was to take care of them. It's the best example of what "win today" means.

We want everyone to ask, "What can I do today that's going to set me up for future success?" We're going to shoot for goals, but ultimately, we have to enjoy the journey, even the rough spots on the road. We enjoy making missteps that ultimately lead to us discovering something that takes us even further into improvement because that's how you learn to grow and be better. Sometimes it's easy for people to get frustrated or feel down because they didn't hit the goal or because it's too late in the month and they can't hit the goal. My job is to get them to take a step back and understand that we're going to be fine— just take it one call at a time, and take care of this customer. We're always encouraging this way of thinking because it's easy to become trapped in negative thinking and not focus on the moment.

Recognize Your Team Members' Successes

We use our monthly all-company meetings to regularly acknowledge our people's successes and relate their success to the company's success. Employees receive awards every month, and leadership determines the winners with input from the managers. Some of these awards are for the employees of the month, the installation of the month, and the top producers of the month. The employees compete against each other through customer reviews. For the Installation of the Month Award, all of the installers take before-and-after photos of their jobs and send them in to the competition. We pick three finalists, and then the whole group votes for who they think has the install of the month. The awards we give are part of the fun. For example, we make up some goofy trophies for the employees of the month, and the top producers get a wrestling belt.

The competitions are just one way to recognize employees for their hard work, but they're also a lot of fun for everyone. When we first started the contests, I wondered who would put the whole program together and if we even needed to make the effort. But after we held the competitions for several months, I wondered why we hadn't been doing it all along. We always talked about wanting employees to improve themselves and their work, but I realized we never told them they'd done an awesome job. Such initiatives reinforce our company's core values and the central principles of our culture, both of which are crucial to keeping a culture thriving. As anyone who's trying to go after a big goal knows, you must have some small victories to keep the momentum going, and you have to take time to celebrate those victories, no matter how big or small.

Leaders who want to start similar programs to recognize employees' achievements should remember that recognition is about the small things as well as the big wins. Many leaders might not think the little things are important. But if you want to be a great leader and keep the cadence of culture on a steady beat, you have to show people that you appreciate everything they do, no matter how small. Recognizing just one person for a job well done can greatly influence everyone in the company. They see that they're working with good people who are achieving, and that gets them excited. Most important, we make it fun. I'm a pretty serious person, but I know that people like to have fun. We try to have as much fun as we can at company meetings because people need that diversion. They enjoy contests and competitions to cheer each other on, but they also know that their hard work grows the company and their opportunities. Everyone always tries to do better in that kind of atmosphere, and everyone wins. Peterman isn't a company full of individual positions in different departments—it's a team, and our culture celebrates success as a team and acknowledges those who are doing a great job.

Keep Your Door Open

My door is always open, especially in the morning when people are bustling in and out of the facility. I enjoy talking casually with the different people who pop into the office throughout the day. But I mostly want to have little conversations to find out how people are getting along and what's going on in their lives and to make sure that we're doing right by them here at work. Talking with people is the best way I know to show you care. Many of our people come into the office only occasionally because they work in the field, but when they come in on meeting days, for example, I always make it a point to talk with them to see how they're doing. I might not have seen them for a week because they're always out on calls, but I make the effort to acknowledge that we care about them. I might ask them about their recent vacations or how their kids are doing in school. It's the human aspect that I think sometimes gets lost in business because leaders are focused too much on revenue and numbers. If I focus on only the numbers when I interact with our people, they'll probably focus only on the numbers when they're at a customer's house, and that doesn't make for a good customer experience.

Someone once asked me how I keep those little conversations from sounding superficial. The question surprised me because I've never had trouble making small talk with others, though I know that some people find small talk difficult. My conversations are genuine because I actually do care about what's going on with our people. When I ask someone how their family is doing, I truly want to know.

It goes back to understanding our purpose, which is to have an impact on people every day. If I'm superficial in any way in my conversations, then I'm not being true to myself, who I want to be, and what our company stands for. Many business owners say they want to build a great culture, but they're not willing to take the steps necessary to do it. Their conversations are probably superficial because they're not doing what it takes to get to know somebody or to build a real relationship. Again, they're concerned with only the numbers and not the relationships, and you must care about relationships. Ultimately, true caring helps grow the person, and that person will take a bigger, more vested interest in the company as a whole.

Constantly Hire for Your Culture

Hiring the best employees we can find is important to keeping our culture alive and the cadence steady. We want to attract people who will fit into our culture and thrive in it. To that end, we see the recruiting process as a way for us to sell ourselves to prospective employees almost more than they're trying to sell themselves to us. We're setting the stage and the expectations so that the prospects understand what kind of company they'll join, which we think is unlike anything else they might have experienced in our industry.

> Hiring the best employees we can find is important to keeping our culture alive and the cadence steady.

As companies grow, leadership can feel pressured to hire people quickly to meet demands, and they might give in to a feeling that they just need to hire someone without considering whether they'll fit into the company culture. It's a big mistake that could affect the company for a long time. It's always important to hire (and even fire) based on your company culture—that is, your shared goals and values—especially when you're growing quickly. You can teach new hires the skills they need to succeed on the job, but you can't teach values. Hiring the wrong people can create a negative feeling in the workplace and even cost you money in the end because you'll have to hire repeatedly to replace failed employees who don't share your values.

For example, we hire many highly skilled and experienced people, but hiring the best means we even take a close look at people who don't have any experience whatsoever because they might be a perfect cultural fit. We sometimes hire technicians who want to get into the trades and learn a skill—it's the concept of apprenticeship. They learn things through experience from an older, more experienced person who takes them under their wing and shows them the ropes. In these cases, we hire for character—good people who want to serve others and take care of the customer and who aren't afraid to ask questions. We can teach them skills, but their character must fit in with our culture.

Peterman's Hiring Process

Hiring the best is great for the company, but it's the best service we offer our customers too. When they call on us to solve their problems, they know that the best of the best will be coming to their homes. The customer trusts us to do this. Our hiring process is somewhat different from most companies in our industry because we use two ways to find the best people to hire.

- **Internal referral program.** We believe that if we hire the best, the best usually associate with other people who are at the tops of their fields. We created an internal referral program that pays the employee $100 if they refer somebody who goes through our phone interview process and comes in for an in-person interview. I'm sure many companies have employee referral programs, but here's how ours is different: our employee is "tied" to the person they referred to us. If we hire that person and they stay for ninety days, we pay the referring employee $150 a month for as long as that person works here for up to five years. This is an amazing employee benefit and motivator, and we hire many good people through this program.

- **Always recruiting.** We're constantly looking for people and reaching out to interview prospects for all positions in the company. We have to recruit and interview prospects all the time if we want to have the best people on our teams. We might not even have an open position, but I believe that constantly recruiting is an opportunity to find the right employee—someone who's highly skilled but who's also a good fit for our company culture. I try to be in on almost every job interview, at least the first or second interview.

Leadership and management are heavily involved in our hiring process. Often, one of our managers talks, or I talk, with the candidates during their first interview to determine if they'll be a good fit at Peterman. We ask many questions to find specific characteristics in people. Here are just a few of the characteristics we seek in job candidates:

- Ability to lead themselves. We ask, "Are you taking responsibility for yourself?" We're looking for people who are already leading themselves, exhibit some of the qualities of leading themselves, or are working on it. We've found that people who can lead themselves are much easier to teach and are far more receptive to coaching.

- Not self-absorbed. We want people who want to be part of a team, and that means caring about each other. A self-absorbed person cares more about themselves than they care about others, and someone like that won't work well on a team.
- General care and compassion. This is a big part of our culture, and someone won't fit in if they don't have these traits.
- Communicates well with people and is outgoing. Our business is residential, and our people must interact with customers every day. They're the face of our company in our customers' homes, so they must be able to communicate and form good relationships with people.

Finding these different characteristics in a person isn't as easy as reading skills and experience on a résumé. We use example-based questions to get to these traits. Here are some examples:

- Tell me about a time when you were part of a team. What role did you play, and what role do you like to play on a team?
- Tell me about something that made you proud.
- What types of things do you do for fun?
- Tell me about a time when you helped a new employee who was struggling.

Questions such as these tell us a lot about how someone might or might not fit in with our culture. We also might ask preference questions because some tradespeople might come from commercial settings in which they generally don't have much interaction with people—an apartment setting, for example, where they do the work while the tenant is out and where they don't really have a customer.

So we might ask, Do you prefer working in a setting dealing with customers or one in which you don't interact with customers?

We also include some of our employees in the interviews, usually three people and at least one male and one female. They are there to observe how the candidates react to the questions we ask because we trust our employees' good sense for who will or won't fit in with our culture. After the interview, we discuss the candidates and focus on several important points, such as, Would you feel comfortable if this person walked into your house? Our trust in our employees' judgment runs deep. One of our people stopped a candidate at the door because of how he greeted her and his unkempt appearance. She had such a strong sense that he wouldn't fit in at Peterman because of those two things, and we were fine with that. We'll usually hire someone who gets a thumbs-up from our employee observers, and those candidates who join the family move on to our orientation day.

Orientation Day

New hires go through a full day of orientation in which they learn about our mission and review our Vivid Vision statement. This is the best way for them to learn about the company, our background, and our goals. Many of our managers speak to the new recruits, and we show them several videos we made about the company and our people. The orientation is a full day of immersing them in our culture, what we do and how we do it, and showing them that Peterman is a special place to work. The orientation cements the notion that we're family owned and all employees are family. They learn that we in leadership aren't strangers, and they can talk with us any time they want. Leadership has the chance to get to know people with whom we might not interact daily, but we intend to maintain a connection.

DiSC Profile Assessment

New hires take an assessment called the DiSC profile, which helps us understand how that person communicates and learns. Leaders need this information so they can communicate and respond to people in effective ways based on the person's individuality as a leader. You have to be someone a little bit different for each individual person. For example, some people are visual learners, while others are auditory learners. Knowing this information helps us manage people better and communicate with them effectively. We don't use this assessment to hire people but to find out how they learn and communicate after we've hired them. This tool has been effective in improving our relationships and interactions with our people.

Hiring for your culture becomes easier when you understand whom you're looking for. I think many companies experience hiring issues because they're unsure of who they are as a company, so they can't know what they want in their employees and can't pinpoint someone who will be a good fit. I've found that the clearer we've become on what our culture needs to be and what our goals are for our people and our customers, the better we became at hiring because we know exactly who will fit in and who won't. Sometimes we still swing and miss, so we're not perfect, but I think our success comes from not being afraid to swing and miss.

Keep Your Finger on the Pulse of Your Company

Leaders must constantly have a finger on the pulse of the organization if they want to keep the cadence of culture steady. We conduct employee surveys twice a year, and we take these surveys seriously.

Some companies conduct surveys but then don't do anything with what they learn from the results. I think it would be naive to conduct the survey and ignore the results—it's a recipe for disaster because everyone's concerns are important.

Surveys give employees a voice and a way to give leadership constructive feedback. This emphasizes the importance of the employees' role in the company and shows that leadership values their opinions. Leadership can use surveys to set objectives for change and to find out what we're doing right in the company. For example, if a specific department is doing exceptionally well, leadership can look closely at how they're achieving their success and develop best practices to use elsewhere in the company. Surveys provide valuable data to use to further the company's growth.

Our surveys focus on several areas but especially on the employees themselves. For example, we ask if they believe they have a career path, if they feel supported in their careers, and if they think the company has a bigger vision. If anyone says they don't feel supported or can't see their future in the company, we have to address that situation right away. Our prompt attention to issues raised in surveys is another way of showing employees that we care about them, so they're also more inclined to give us honest feedback.

Besides the surveys, I'm always talking with people to make sure everything's okay with them and asking for feedback. I learn a lot from our people because they're honest with me. We've created an atmosphere in which they know that leadership takes their views and opinions seriously, so they're not afraid to tell us the truth. Our winning atmosphere keeps the cadence of our culture steadily beating.

A Winning Atmosphere

One night as I was driving home, my phone was buzzing with text messages in a group text with technicians from one of our departments. I pulled over to read the messages, and they were telling each other what a good job someone did or bragging about something they sold. They were also answering questions and helping each other, encouraging each other. I thought to myself, "This is so cool—*this* is what Peterman is all about!" Those guys were truly having fun doing what they do, but to me, camaraderie was the most important thing I saw in those texts. They spend their days helping people and know that they're doing it for the right reasons, but they're doing it as part of a group, and they love being part of that group.

Ultimately, that's my job as their leader: to create the right atmosphere for them, make sure everyone knows we care about them, and make sure they're having fun while doing a good job. When all that is present, it shows that our culture is thriving and the steady beat of the cadence is ongoing. The customer wins, the employees win, and the company wins.

Chapter 6:

Give Them a Voice and a Choice

Chris from Peterman saved our holiday and birthday weekend! We called over ten plumbing companies, and Peterman was the only one that was able to get a plumber out within two hours. Chris was kind, transparent, professional, and knowledgeable! Awesome to have someone with twenty-seven years of experience take the time to explain elementary aspects of his field ... supernice and humble guy! He kindly explained the few different types of pumps we had in our basement, educated us on how everything works, and was in/out in an hour or so. We are scheduling him back to update one of our other older pumps. All transactions were done on an iPad including the equipment options. Very thankful he was able to get in so quickly and change out the ejector (sewage) pump ... we were a half inch of pit space left from a ruined basement. Call these guys for all your needs ... emergency, ongoing maintenance, and for replacement/upgrade items! Thank you!

—Frank K.

Peterman's philosophy centers on the fact that our industry often gets a bad name from customers' expectations of a low level of service. My dad set out to break the mold when he started this company. For him (and for me and all of us at Peterman today), the relationship with the customer starts and ends with good communication and an overall respect for a customer's home—from the office, the technician, the installation crew, and everyone in the company.

I used to hear many stories about customer dissatisfaction in our industry, and often dissatisfaction arises when two factors are missing in a company-customer relationship: voice and choice. When those are missing, the result is usually dissatisfied customers in any industry. In fact, we find that many customers are actually used to poor service and come to expect it.

What do we mean by voice and choice? In our context, it's how you can personalize your service and become a customer-focused business. It's opening communication and providing customers with ways to have their say, whether by soliciting feedback (through surveys, for example), asking for reviews, or ensuring that customers know you'll listen if they want to talk with you. Giving them a choice means providing options in products and services—quality products at different price levels, for example, or repair options to suit budgets and schedules. We've embraced the concept of voice and choice because it fits perfectly with Dad's goals of maintaining good communication and respect for customers, and it's the epitome of what it means to be customer focused.

Becoming Customer Focused

We're in the business of taking care of people, and it's our job to go above and beyond for our customers. Many businesses, however, put their primary focus on money, and both the customers and their employees are nothing more than a source of money. Customer-focused companies don't think of employees and customers as the money source. Instead, they treat employees as their number-one customer, and those employees take care of the customers. We've found this to be true. Companies will have trouble satisfying customers if they don't treat their employees right, if the workplace isn't fun for people and they don't like being there, and especially if employees feel like they're not appreciated. This is a people business, and if people don't feel appreciated, they won't perform, which in this case means they won't take care of the customer the way they should. We treat our people like they're the best in this industry, make sure they know that we care about them, and give our company a higher purpose that employees can believe in, and they take care of our customers every single time. The company takes care of employees, employees take care of customers, customers pay for advice from employees; then the company makes money and grows, and the company can take care of employees—it's a big circle, and everybody wins. Focusing on employees first, therefore, leads to an overall customer focus throughout the company.

> Focusing on employees first, therefore, leads to an overall customer focus throughout the company.

Business owners who implement strategies like ours or similar strategies need to monitor the strategies to determine if they're working to create a positive company-employee relationship. The best way to find out is to survey your employees. We conduct employee surveys twice a year to learn from the results, particularly those relating to the employees personally. I recommend surveying employees at least that often. If the surveys tell you that your employees feel appreciated, then you're on the right path, but if they don't, you've likely found your problem. Dwindling or low customer satisfaction is almost always a sign that many of your employees—if not most—feel unappreciated. If that's the case, you need to make changes.

I find it hard to believe that employees who are excited about their jobs and their company could ever provide subpar service. Happy employees will do anything they can to help make the company successful.

Voice and Choice Means Personalized Service

Ultimately, personalizing your service lies in having a good balance of voice and choice. I believe that other businesses in our industry fall down a bit on this point. Many don't communicate well with customers or give them a voice, yet customer feedback is essential for any company to grow and improve. At Peterman, we make it very easy for customers to leave feedback because the more we learn about our performance, the more we can improve. We respond to every review and thank the customer for their time. As of this writing, we have more than a thousand Google reviews between our three locations, and we value each one of these.

Customers know that you respect them when you listen to them, even if (and especially if) they have a complaint. Being unresponsive is another communications fail. Some businesses think they're too busy to respond, and that's wrong. You can probably remember asking a company for a quote or expecting to have your call returned, but you never got a response. It's not a good feeling, and you might have wondered if the company forgot about you. You might have been very interested in doing business with that company, but because they didn't respond to you, you probably decided to do business with someone else. Sadly, I see a trend in our industry of putting less priority on communication and making sure that customers know where they stand. Every customer is important and deserves a response.

Similarly, many companies don't offer customers much choice, particularly regarding repairs. Choice means our technicians never give them just one solution to their problem. In any situation, we present several different options the customer can choose from to correct the problem. It can start with a simple Band-Aid solution to one that might last a little bit longer and up to a permanent solution. I think this is extremely important because it makes the customer partners with us to find a solution instead of us telling them what to do. In this way, we help the customer make the best decision for their home, which is their biggest investment. Whether the solution is short term or long term, customers should choose how to deal with their issues. This gives them a more active role in what could be expensive decisions for their homes. For example, if we're called to a home to fix a leaking water heater and learn that the customer is interested in adding a water softener and maybe a water filtering system, it's a good opportunity to provide choices. Our technician can quote an option for just fixing the problem (the reason we were called out) but could also quote an option for a new water heater, a different kind of water heater (tankless, for example), an option for a regular water heater plus a softener, and an option for all three items. They might decline all options and go with the repair, or they might repair and add equipment. Whatever the case, we guide them through solving their problems and educate them on potential solutions.

Businesses can use creativity to come up with ways of giving customers voice and choice. Over the years, our experience led us to develop several customer programs that have worked well for us and made Peterman stand out in the industry. I'll describe these programs so you can see how they work and perhaps get inspiration to develop similar programs for your business.

Building Relationships with Customers: The Peterman Difference

I've found that most problems in our industry usually involve miscommunication. In building good relationships with customers, we try to overcommunicate to make sure everyone understands what's happening with the job. If a customer has a problem they feel is big enough to take to the top, they can use our Owner's Voice Guarantee—one of several guarantees we give our customers (and another good way to build strong, lasting customer relationships). We guarantee that if a customer is dissatisfied with our service for any reason and wants to talk with one of the owners, all they have to do is call and ask for one of us named Peterman, and we'll talk with them to solve the issue. I'm proud that I don't get many such requests, but if I do, miscommunication is generally the cause. Maybe we haven't explained the situation properly, or the customer had an impression about the situation but was told something different. For example, the customer might say they talked with the technician and was told something, which was the technician's way of thinking. The technician wasn't trying to mislead the customer, and it just came down to one person not understanding the other. My job is to sort through such misunderstandings, and I take responsibility for the issue just by talking with the customer. When I understand the problem fully, I explain what was going on and do whatever I can to get the job back on track to the customer's satisfaction.

I like this particular guarantee because it emphasizes voice on both sides. We encourage our customers to use their voices and guarantee that we will use our voices to solve their problems instead of making excuses or ignoring them completely. In an industry that often deemphasizes communication, our commitment shows that we want don't want to take advantage of anybody (and I can say that we've never taken advantage of anybody). Customers just want to know that they're not getting swept under the rug and that their issues are important. When our customers know they can call on us any time, that's often all they want and need to hear.

Listening to Customers

Communicating with customers means more than just us giving our customers information. We also need to listen to what our customers tell us. Everyone has probably felt that a company they hired wasn't really listening to them, even if the technician says, "I hear you." At this point, I think it's important to understand the difference between hearing and listening. Hearing is passive—it's something you do without trying. For example, your lawn maintenance company might be outside right now using leaf blowers, and you can hear those blowers without trying to hear them. Listening, however, is an active, conscious effort, something you choose to do. When listening, you pay attention to what you hear, and it requires concentration so that your brain processes meaning from words and sentences. Listening is actually a learned skill, and it leads to learning. As a leader, you should encourage a desire to listen in your people. Because listening is a conscious choice, your people in the field must *want* to listen to customers. By listening to customers,

> When our customers know they can call on us any time, that's often all they want and need to hear.

they can uncover what's important to them and what's going to be a win for them.

TIPS TO PROMOTE BETTER LISTENING

- Avoid distractions when you need to listen. Focus on the speaker (the customer) to really hear what they're saying.

- Put the customer at ease. Relax and look at the person speaking to help them feel free to talk.

- Don't be quick to judge what's said. Wait until the customer is finished speaking. Listen to everything they have to say before processing it.

- Understand the customer's point of view. Remember that the customer lives in the home and is living with the problems that affect life in the home. They might be understandably upset or anxious.

How do you know if your people in the field are really listening to customers? One way to find out is to send your managers out in the field observe how your people communicate with customers. We always encourage our managers to do ride-alongs with the technicians to make sure that we're communicating effectively. Although listening to customers seems like common sense, we also have to recognize that as professionals, listening means listening for what's *not* being said, and then we need to ask questions to clarify the meaning of words and the feelings involved. Knowing what questions to ask is sometimes the bigger challenge that we face, and we need to teach our team members what questions to ask.

I think we can always improve how we listen to our customers. Sometimes customers say things indirectly, and we need to find out what they're trying to say by really listening. Are they scared? Are they uneducated, or have we not educated them enough? Whatever the case may be, we need to figure that out by asking great questions and then listening—not listening for what we want to hear but rather listening for what the customer's telling us is wrong or how the customer is trying to explain what's confusing them. We listen first and speak second, and then we can solve the actual problem instead of just telling them our own perspective on what the problem is and what the customer needs.

Customers call us for our expertise, but if we can't ask the right questions to draw answers from the customers, then we can't really help them. We teach our people how to ask questions, and though it might seem funny to say that we teach them how to ask questions, we've developed an entire process that aims primarily at making the customer feel comfortable. We always want customers to feel comfortable because they won't feel like we're trying to take advantage of them, and it makes it easier for them to explain their problem. For example, it's important for us to understand how a customer uses their home in a particular instance—the heating system and the plumbing system can be unique to how a homeowner uses them. Often a technician goes to a home and assumes that a fix-all solution will take care of the problem. But depending on how the homeowner uses their home, the fix-all solution might not work for them. We need to do a very good job of talking to the customer, asking the questions in a way that helps them uncover what the problem actually is, and then giving them a voice. I believe that we empower customers by asking questions, exploring the home and how they use it, and really taking an interest in helping them.

Building relationships takes commitment, creativity, and a willingness to take a little risk. By risk, I mean offering the customer a lot and trusting them not to take advantage of you. We offer our customers a wide range of service benefits and options—some are unique in the industry, some are rare, and others might be common, but we put an extra twist on it to make it special.

The Peterman Protection Club

We give our customers choices and real value through a program we call the Peterman Protection Club. The customer can buy into a plan of guarantees and benefits that cover many issues, such as burst pipes, broken air conditioners, clogged drains, or broken hot-water heaters, but it goes further. Our plan covers customers' problems 24/7 and gives peace of mind in stressful situations, such as when problems occur late at night or on weekends, when other companies might charge extra fees. Our customers love the plan because it also saves them time and money.

Well-designed plans that give customers both voice and choice are good for your business too. They provide recurring income, develop customer loyalty, increase trust, teach your customers the benefits of routine maintenance, and keep you in touch with customers regularly, so you might gain additional work. Additionally, you might reduce your marketing expenses because you'll have less need to acquire new customers.

Here's what several of our satisfied customer have said about the Peterman Protection Club:

> *"One thing I enjoy is the Peterman Protection Club. Dealing with other companies and contractors for home repair and*

maintenance, I've found that trust, for me personally, is the number-one priority, followed by price. I think with Peterman, you're getting the best of both worlds."

"The club charges a monthly fee, and it's a twenty-four-hour service. It's peace of mind, and working with a service company like Peterman is like nothing I've ever encountered."

"Peterman explained that they would come out at least twice annually to do a full system inspection, not only of heating and cooling, but also plumbing. It's a small monthly payment, and it gives us great peace of mind throughout the year."

"Joining the Peterman Protection Club seemed like a no-brainer. Even if you take the monthly fee times twelve, if you have one or two service calls, you're going to save money."

"It saved me a substantial amount of money off of my repair bill, and now I can have service done on my plumbing, heating, and air-conditioning throughout the year."

"It gives us peace of mind knowing that if something goes wrong, Peterman can come and take care of it in a timely manner and for a reasonable price."

Our plan is popular, but if customers are undecided about joining the club, we offer them a trial run. We let our technicians show them the value of protection they can trust from Peterman.

Customers who need service are usually afraid of three things when they need to choose a company: being dissatisfied, not getting the value they wanted, and losing their money. Smart companies will give customers good reasons to choose their services over others. Guarantees—standing behind your work with a promise of quality—can ensure that your company stands out in the crowd and increases trust, even with people who've never called on you before. A guarantee means you're confident you can solve their problems. Your potential for reward is higher than your risk, but only if you have trust in your people and stand behind your work 110 percent, like we do.

Designing plans that give your customers good choices takes time and creativity. What kind of guarantees could your company offer? For some examples, the Peterman Protection Plan offers these guarantees:

"Owner's Voice" Guarantee

Our customers have direct access to me to discuss any issue, and we won't hide behind layers of management or made-up excuses. We're a family-owned company that treats all of our customers like family.

"We Value Your Time" Guarantee

Our call center is open twenty-four hours a day, seven days a week, and when our customers call, they will always speak with a live person. Our experienced customer service representatives will schedule an appointment that's convenient for the customer. We call before our technician arrives so customers don't waste time waiting for us. Also, we send the customer an email with the technician's picture and biography so they know who will be showing up at their door.

"We Value Your Home" Guarantee

Our technicians use floor-protecting shoe covers and drop cloths to protect our customers' homes and make sure to leave the interiors of their houses in the same condition they were in before they arrived. If customers aren't satisfied, we'll clean the home.

"TELL-A-FRIEND" Guarantee

We agree to accept responsibility for making sure customers are satisfied but also feel confident enough to tell a friend about our company. If the customer is dissatisfied with our service or our people for any reason and would not consider telling a friend about our company, we'll do whatever it takes to make it right and correct the problem.

"One-Year Test Drive" Guarantee

If a customer is ever unhappy with an installation and we can't fix it, we'll remove the system and refund 100 percent of the customer's original investment at any time during the first year—no ifs, ands, or buts.

"Five-Star Service" Guarantee

This guarantee states that our technicians are the best in their skills, attitude, and workmanship. We provide extensive training to keep them up to date on new market developments, which means that customers will have the most knowledgeable technicians in the industry coming to their homes. They'll take care of the home, complete jobs promptly and with precision, clean up when they're finished, and take personal responsibility for the customer's satisfaction. Every technician has had a background check and drug screening. If a technician doesn't perform within our high standards, we'll do everything in our power to correct the situation and make it right.

Along with the guarantees, the Peterman Protection Plan offers these services as club member benefits:

Air Conditioner Outdoor Coil Cleaning

Air conditioner coils are cleaned to perfection, and we change out the dirty filter.

Furnace Twenty-Two-Point Inspection

This is a top-to-bottom safety check to make sure the furnace is safe and protect our customers from potential poisonous gas leaks.

Furnace Performance Report

Hairline cracks in furnaces that can emit harmful gases often go unnoticed. We check gas levels before and after service and document it for safety.

Whole House Plumbing Inspection

Our plumbers perform a 103-point inspection to catch plumbing problems before they start.

Plumbing Bonus! Safety Valve Tags

We tag shutoff valves for quick identification in emergencies.

Chore of Your Choice

Our unique service helps customers with small chores just because we can and we care. As long as our technician is at the house, why not ask him or her change a light bulb, take the trash out, or bring in the newspaper? All our customers have to do is ask.

Helping You Help Others: Service Project of the Month

From fundraisers to clothing and food drives, we are partners in the community with our customers.

We also create great customer relationships by offering up-front pricing (not charging time and material), payment options (which is uncommon in our industry), a dedicated customer care representative to resolve customer issues and ensure satisfaction, and a charity donation of $5 to a customer's favorite charity when they make a repair with us. Also, we don't charge a service fee for club members (normally $85). The Peterman Protection Club speaks for itself with its benefits and guarantees, but we add so much more to build the best customer relationships possible. I think many businesses are afraid to give customers guarantees or incentives, sometimes because they think they might have to honor them and they can't afford to do that. I know that seems odd, but maybe those businesses don't have enough faith and trust in their employees and their company mission to stand behind a guarantee. You must have great confidence in your employees and your company's work to offer guarantees.

> The Peterman Protection Club speaks for itself with its benefits and guarantees, but we add so much more to build the best customer relationships possible.

Peterman Party

You've read about our company gatherings and how much fun we have together along with our hard work, but a Peterman party isn't about company gatherings. In fact, we don't like to have this type of party, but sometimes it's necessary. A Peterman party is a serious process that we initiate if a customer has a problem that requires us to go to their home multiple times. I mention it here because we consider it both a benefit and a guarantee for the customer, even though we don't list this benefit in any of our materials or even tell customers about it unless it's needed (and our goal is to never have to use it). But if a situation arises, we pull out all of the stops.

Here's a scenario: our technician went out to the home, the work wasn't done properly for some reason, we sent another technician, and the issue still wasn't fixed. We call for a Peterman party: the first technician, the service manager, the installation manager, my brother or me, and sometimes an installer who visits the home again—at least four highly qualified people from our company go to the customer's home and will fix the problem for the last time. The customer's immediate reaction is usually surprise and a bit of confusion because no company had ever responded to them like this before. But once they understand what is happening and why, they are really impressed. I don't think we've ever left a Peterman party with the customer not impressed by the level of service provided and understanding that our company is serious about fixing their issue. I'm happy to say that we don't have Peterman parties very often, and I haven't been out on many of these parties, but if we do need to have one, it's usually because the problem is a weird or unique issue. Our customers are very impressed with the results and with the knowledge that we weren't going to leave until we fixed the problem.

Things can go wrong in the best of companies. A misunderstanding, a bad piece of equipment, or a bad replacement part could be the cause, but a company that has its act together can manage when things go wrong. We jump in and make a bad situation right, whatever it takes. In fact, when things go wrong, we think it's our time to shine. I challenge everyone to raise our game when we have to correct a mistake. For example, in our business, a warranty call usually means the customer goes to the back of the line because the company won't make any money on such calls. We do the opposite and instead send dedicated technicians who take care of these calls.

We believe that if a customer has an issue, we don't always have to win, and we'll overdeliver on making it right. Customers will remember your willingness to overcompensate them for a bad experience and will never leave you.

VOICE AND CHOICE: TIPS TO GET IT RIGHT

- Give your customers a voice by using your voice to communicate. We might overcommunicate in some instances, but we want to make sure we respect our customer's time, so we explain everything in great detail to avoid any possible confusion.

- Listen to your customers. Our technicians explore the home with the homeowner and listen to them so we can do a better job of protecting their homes. We usually go wrong if we try to sell them something instead of just taking care of them—that's when no one wins.

- Win, win, win. Make sure your customer wins rather than just the technician and the company. The best way to make sure customers win is to listen for what they actually want.

- Stand behind your work. Last year we misdiagnosed something and recommended replacing the system. When installing the system, we learned about something that was done wrong from the start. We ended up giving the customer her money back, *and* she got a new system.

- Do whatever it takes to be there for your customers. In our industry, customer service is twenty-four hours a day, and we give our customers a voice by letting them use theirs to call us for service at any time. When they call us, they'll always talk with a live person, and we always have a technician ready to respond. It doesn't make any sense to protect customers' homes only during normal business hours. We build trust with our customers because they know they can always call us if something goes wrong. Other businesses might think that it's a nuisance if customers can call at all hours of the night, but we want our customers to call us. If we aren't available, they might be forced to call someone else who might not provide good service and would charge them more. If that happens, then we're not protecting them at all.

- Underpromise and overdeliver. Considering our industry's reputation for doing the opposite, always following this strategy is a sure win for everyone.

- Be consistent with your service. Good customer service starts with making sure you follow a system, and a good system will allow you to do the job right every time. You should see consistency in your service, regardless of who is out at your customer's home.

- Allow customers to demand higher levels of service. Some people get irritated when customers demand service that seems like it's far above and beyond the norm, but we view this as an honor. We might not be able to meet all of their expectations, but giving our customers a voice in this way forces us to find our flaws and improve.

- Remember that everything is in the follow-up. You have to have someone in your business who is in charge of responding when customers use their voices—at least one person who can answer questions for the customer and make sure they know you care about their project. Our production coordinator follows up on every estimate we give. Isn't it frustrating to get a proposal from someone and then never hear from them again? We make sure this doesn't happen. Even if the customer isn't going to buy right then and there, we want to be there for them through the entire buying decision, regardless of how it develops.

- Aim to be the best. If you're not trying to improve your operation, your business will fail, and then you can't take care of your customer. We're constantly looking for ways to invest in things that make our customers' lives easier. Whether it's adding services, providing customers with technician bios, or texting us for service, being creative with our offerings and how we operate lets us stand above the rest, and our customers notice and appreciate it.

Chapter 7:

Give Your Service Real Significance

I called and had a lot of estimates from different companies. While Peterman was not the cheapest, they were also not the most expensive; however their customer service, their respect, and the fact they redid all of my plumbing speaks volumes. Very courteous, very professional, and the team that assembled my shower made something fit where measurement-wise it would not. Not only did it look good, it worked with no leaks. Beyond question the best plumbing company, hands down.

—Robert S.

"Service with significance" is service directed toward another's benefit. For your customers, this means they feel the service they receive is personal and has real value for them. It also applies to your employees, who must feel that they benefit from providing great service. Peterman's philosophy of treating our team members as our number-one customers ensures that they'll take care of our customers every time. Both the company and the employees benefit from this cycle. We've learned that to provide service with significance, there are things you need to do inside your business to encourage your people to provide that service while encouraging your customers to expect that service.

Mindset: Helping the Customer

It's no secret that our industry often has a bad reputation that usually comes from companies taking advantage of customers. I believe one reason this happens is that a company's employees are incentivized to do so (for example, technicians being rewarded for how much they can sell to customers). If selling products or making repairs are the primary focus of how a company operates, they're ignoring the most important thing that leads to a win for everyone involved: helping the customer. This is why companies like ours are in business in the first place. A mindset of helping the customer not only creates wins for the company, the team member, and the customer, but it also is the key to service with significance. We address this in our training at Peterman, and we call this the "repair, sales, help" concept.

> A mindset of helping the customer not only creates wins for the company, the team member, and the customer, but it also is the key to service with significance.

When teaching technicians how to run a service call and how to provide the best customer service possible, our trainer asks: How many of you take on the role of repair person when going to a customer's home? This means going to the home with a mindset of repairing something to get the customer's system back up and running. The problem with this mindset is that a repair might not be the best thing for the customer, and it might not be what's truly needed. But because the technician has this mindset, he or she is not really diagnosing the customer's problem to the best of his or her ability. The technician is focused on one thing: repair the system.

Then the trainer asks: How many of you get calls for which the call notes say the air conditioner isn't working, and the first thing you think is that you're going to go out there and sell them something? With the sales mindset, the technician plans to sell the customer a new part, a new unit, or perhaps a protection plan. Again, this might not be best for the customer in this particular situation, but selling something becomes the technician's goal, and that's what he or she wants to do.

Finally, the trainer asks: How many of you go out there with the sole objective of helping your customer? This is the all-important question, and in the end, all technicians should raise their hands when asked this question. We try to teach all of our technicians that they need to go into the call with no objective other than to help the customer. If they go out there with a mindset of repairing a unit or selling something, maybe for that customer and their situation, the better solution is to replace the unit. But the technician can't see that solution because they've already determined that repairing or selling is the solution, and they did that before they even arrived at the customer's home. Many times, repairing or selling is the wrong solution, and in those cases, no one wins.

When you come from a place of just wanting to help the customer, there's no right or wrong solution. There might be several different ways to fix the problem. It's up to the technicians to uncover, by listening to the customer, what's important to them and what he or she can do to make the situation a win for everyone. To do that, the technician needs to have the right mindset: helping the customer. You're there to offer your help in making a decision to get the problem fixed today, and by doing so, you're truly providing service with significance.

Here's a real-life example: we had a situation once in which a technician was out at a customer's home and recommended an expensive repair, which the customer agreed to do. However, we received a call back to the customer's home a few months later, and they were upset because they'd made the expensive repair, but it wasn't working any longer. We looked back at the customer's service history and could see that the technician provided the customer with only one option: repair the unit. Did he talk with the homeowner about replacing? We figured he probably mentioned it, but he didn't follow through with it as a serious option by writing it down for the customer to see. In my mind, he didn't give them the option to replace. So we were stuck in a situation in which the customer was upset because they felt they wouldn't have spent the money on the repair if there was even a chance the repair would break down three months later. It was clear that if given the option to replace, the customer would have taken it.

In this case, we went out of our way to take care of the customer. We credited back the cost of the repair and then replaced the unit the next week. I felt this was the right thing to do because we didn't provide the best service for that customer. Unfortunately, going out to the home with a repair mentality often means the technician and the company get a win, but the customer doesn't.

We talked with the technician afterward to discuss the situation and learned that he wasn't really sure what to do at the time. Because of the unit's age, either repairing or replacing were reasonable. However, we felt and noted to him that he came from a mindset of repairing only, and if he had a mindset of just helping a customer, then he would have uncovered what was truly a win for that customer and explained all the options. Later, if that customer made a repair, and on that ticket it also had an option for replacement, we could have reminded the customer that he chose to repair even though he was given an option to replace. We would have asked if there was a reason he opted not to replace originally. At that point, it's a different conversation, and the customer's no longer upset.

This was very enlightening for that technician, and he was extremely disappointed in himself for not giving the customer all possible options. He even said, "Well, I guess I'm kind of getting in my own way, aren't I?" We told him what we now teach everyone: when you're going out to a call, come from a place of just wanting to help. You don't have to diagnose it over the phone; you don't have to be Superman. You just have to want to help the customer. If your mind and your heart are in the right place when it comes to helping someone, you're going to help them nine times out of ten, maybe always. To me, that's the essence of what listening to the customer and giving them a voice is all about. The mindset has to be that we're here to help the customer and offer all of the solutions that we know are possible so that they can determine what's best for them and then move forward with the solution.

Measurement and Accountability

Holding each other accountable, setting goals, and striving to be better ultimately result in us providing better service. So it's important to create good service-measurement systems and accountability. Customers hold businesses accountable for the services they provide, and a company that's holding itself and its people accountable is probably going to provide a better service experience. Peterman uses two strategies for accountability. One is our weekly management meeting, in which all of our managers get together to review the previous week's performance through metrics, and the other is our daily board meeting, which isn't a board of directors meeting but rather a meeting about the metrics where we actually write them all on a board. Both of these meetings accomplish two things: everybody who needs to know about our performance is updated on our performance metrics regularly, and plans are made for how to fix problems and improve performance.

Weekly Management Meeting

The weekly management meeting is an idea inspired by Alan Mulally, an engineer and former chief executive officer of Ford Motor Company. He had a concept he called the "working together principle," which is one of twelve principles he says a company can use to "conduct itself, both internally with its employees as well as externally in relation to its customers, suppliers, and community." We studied his style and what he did at Ford to turn it around and customized it to use at Peterman in a similar format. Following his ideas, each department manager is responsible for a set of metrics, and they have five to ten minutes to report on their department's status. The metrics are color coded as a green, yellow, or red light. Green is up to standard. Yellow is not up to standard, but there is a plan to fix it, and

> Customers hold businesses accountable for the services they provide, and a company that's holding itself and its people accountable is probably going to provide a better service experience.

red is not up to standard—it needs special attention, and they're going to need some help.

The meeting's main goal is to inform everyone who needs to know about the metrics being measured. You can probably state four or five different metrics that you're measuring at your company, such as daily sales revenue or the number of new customers you bring into the funnel, for example. But you might not be bringing them to everybody's attention. If only one member of leadership knows those numbers—even when other people affect the numbers—you're going to have trouble improving those metrics. The people who affect the metrics need to know about them, or a leader will be alone in trying to figure out how to fix the red-light problems. Also, putting those metrics out in the open is always good for everyone in the organization. In our case, we're looking at a week's worth of work, and reporting the numbers every week lets us know what a good week looks like and what a bad week looks like. It can be easy for people to just go through the motions when they don't have any concept of what's good and what's bad. But when you can look at metrics and study them, questions come to mind: What did we do that made last week a good one? You begin to find out what works and what doesn't so you can repeat the things that work. Constantly checking in on your performance and the level of service you're providing helps you improve.

Your business can truly grow by fixing the red lights, but your organization's attitude has to embrace the red lights. Instead of getting frustrated and angry and blaming people because red lights even exist, the organization as a whole must look objectively at red lights and see them as learning opportunities and chances to grow and improve. Your leadership and your people need to say, "Hey, that's an area where we can get better." I'm reminded of a podcast I listened to recently in which someone said, "If you're successful, then you're not growing. It's when you fail that you're able to grow." We really do embrace that idea.

I'm not one to flip out whenever we have an issue. Instead, we hold a different kind of meeting we call a special-attention meeting. When we have a red light, we gather all parties who touch the issue in some way, and I go through an exercise called Thinking Time, an idea from entrepreneur and business coach Keith Cunningham. Thinking Time is just what it sounds like: time to think about a problem, an issue, an idea, or a concept. I sit down for half an hour in complete silence and just free think, brainstorming ideas to bring to the table and writing down as many questions as I possibly can about the issue. Some examples of these questions follow: How can we fix this? Whom is this going to affect? Could we fix it [in a specific way]? What would be the biggest problem with doing it this way? Some of these meetings last longer than others, but we really dig into the problem, no matter how long it takes. It's important to get everybody's opinion at these meetings because we might think we have an answer, but then someone might challenge that answer based on their experience. Often, the problem lies in forgetting to involve someone in a process or not bringing an issue to the attention of everybody who needed to know about it—in other words, overlooking a detail. It took a special-attention meeting to discover it, but then the solution to the problem is often very simple.

These weekly meetings are a work in progress. We're not masters of these by any stretch of the imagination, but we've found that simple is better, and you just have to start doing these or something else to start holding yourself accountable. We learn more about how to do these meetings every week. Keeping them simple helps everybody stays on track with what we want to accomplish. Through these meetings, we give our managers a safe environment in which they can examine themselves and their departments objectively, discuss problems and mistakes, and ask for help. If they're struggling with an issue or something's going wrong in their department, everybody is working for a solution together, and we have many great minds at Peterman. We believe that we can fix any issue if we do it together. Just as our customers hold us accountable for our work, we hold each other accountable for making improvements and making the company better for the customer.

Service of significance comes from a company that's willing to hold itself accountable, hold these meetings, have these tough discussions, and figure out how to fix the problems. Give the meetings a try if your business isn't keeping everyone informed about performance metrics. The important thing is to start having such meetings. My best advice to leaders is don't get frustrated. You're not going to develop the best accountability process on your first try. Remember that everybody needs to understand what the metrics mean and why they're important to the overall goal. You can't have a lot of confusing information that only you track and everybody else just kind of glazes over it. Figure out what you need to measure that's meaningful to everyone. Then determine how to get those numbers. Generally, measuring your performance should be easy in your business. Once you uncover your problems, avoiding frustration will ultimately leave you with more time to improve your service and be better for your customers.

Daily Board Meeting

Our second accountability meeting is the daily board meeting. Every day at 9:15 a.m., we meet in a little room that has a whiteboard in it with all of our metrics of interest written on it. Typically, eight people attend this meeting, but anyone in the company can drop in if they want. The board meeting examines everything we did the day before, and we ask ourselves three questions: What do yesterday's numbers look like as of the start of this meeting? How are we trending? Do we need to adjust any of what we're measuring? If we had a bad day, we decide how to turn that around, and if we had a good day, we discuss how to keep the momentum into today. We also discuss that day's prospects based on calls we received between 7:00 a.m. and the meeting time so that our managers can plan the day and make strategic moves rather than reacting all the time. We also look at the budget for the metrics (membership sales, for example) to know whether we're on track.

It's easy to become caught in the whirlwind of business and go for months or even years without measuring performance, and then you wonder why you haven't seen any growth. If you look at numbers monthly, it's too late. You've already made mistakes and likely forgotten details from a month ago that could tell you what went wrong. Weekly and daily checks will allow you to make decisions proactively and provide a high level of service for your customers.

Hiring the Right People

Finding the right people is crucial to providing great service with significance, and it's important for our customers to understand how our company hires. They want a company that has vetted its job candidates thoroughly and ensures that all employees fit with the company culture and values.

We have immediate needs for people that I track on a huge board in my office, but even when a position is filled, we continue to look for candidates. Our hiring process never ends, and it's our mission. We continue looking for candidates even if we don't have open positions. Our goal is to have people lined up out the door waiting to work here, so we continue to interview and build what we call our top five for each position. These are five candidates for each position in the company whom we've interviewed, vetted thoroughly, and deemed as the best to bring on board if and when we need them. Having this bench of quality candidates means we'll never be in a position where we have to hire quickly (and perhaps carelessly) from a place of need.

People always ask, "What if these people go on to take another job at another company?" That's perfectly okay because I'm still going to call them to see what's going on. They might still be at the same job that they didn't like when they first interviewed with us; they might be in a new job that they already know they don't like and could be thinking that they like us better. You just never know the circumstances or what's going on in someone's life at any given time. Sometimes we call people who've taken a job elsewhere, and they like it and are going to stay there, and if that happens, we'll call the number two person on the list and then numbers three, four, and five. Also, just because someone has taken a job elsewhere doesn't mean we take them off of our top-five list. I'll still keep the person in the top five ready candidates but move them down the list to number two and keep checking with him when we have an open position. But I can usually find one person in that list who can jump into an open spot at Peterman. Because we've already qualified that person, we know we're hiring someone who can provide that high level of service with significance. Along with our top five, our employees help us hire good people through referrals. One of our employees referred four people to us, and we ended up hiring all four in one interview.

Because we're always looking for people, our employees are always on their toes. It's like a subtle incentive for everyone to keep performing at their best for the company and the customer. It challenges our people to always improve because there's someone out there who's improving and might want to work for us. My advice to any business is to never stop hiring. We were guilty of doing that in the past—if we needed only one more technician, we'd find him or her, hire that person, and that was the end of the process. But sometimes we'd end up rehiring for that position several more times in the same year because we hired the wrong person. We hired with our fingers crossed under the table, and we should never be in that position or put our customers in a position of receiving service from someone who isn't the most qualified and thoroughly vetted candidate.

Once we hire the best, it's up to us to treat them like the professionals they are by giving them everything they need to do their best work while helping them learn and grow.

Your People Are Professionals

What picture do you get in your mind when you think of a contractor? A common picture in our industry is a guy in an old, rusty white van. Parts fall out of the back when he opens the doors, and the van's dashboard is littered with papers and invoices. Overall, it looks unkempt and is a bad representation. If our service vans looked like this, our customers wouldn't trust us to do a good job in their home, and we wouldn't be successful. I know that something like this can happen when leadership's primary focus for the business is on making money. But I also realized that the technician working from that van has to care too. If he doesn't, it's likely because leadership isn't making him feel like he's the professional that he is.

The Importance of Outward Appearances

The outward signs of professionalism are crucial. Service with significance comes from people who know they're professionals, take pride in all aspects of what they do, and feel that they're partners with your company in providing the best service possible. Peterman's people focus takes care of half that equation, but we also created programs and incentives to make sure that our people know they're professionals and look like it.

Appearances mean a lot in our business because customers must feel comfortable with the people who come into their homes. Peterman's vehicle program replaces our vans every four years on average, and all vans are branded so customers know immediately that our company has arrived at their homes. Keeping our fleet new speaks to our professionalism and shows how we treat our employees. I'm not sending them out in a broken-down beater van because I don't think a technician can provide great service without the best of everything needed to do the job. Our customers have confidence knowing that we won't have to cancel appointments because of vehicle breakdowns, and it shows that we're willing to invest in our technicians and the best equipment.

Our technicians need to have parts to complete customers' jobs in a timely way. Our parts coordinator performs inventory on every van each month, cleaning out the van and counting all the parts to make sure technicians have everything they need for the customer. This is so important because the technicians don't want to find out that they're not prepared to fix the customers' problems. Customers can feel confident that their job will be completed that day because the technician has the parts he needs on board.

Similarly, we have what we call a tool account for our technicians. It essentially sets money aside for them to buy tools. The program started small, providing $200 a year for a technician. Over time, we increased the tool account from $200 a year for a technician to $600 for a lead technician and $450 for an apprentice technician. We think this is important for our people to have what they need to do their jobs right and also for the customer to receive the best possible service from our technicians. Customers don't want technicians trying to fix their expensive investment without the right tools to do it. Similarly, we have another program for young apprentices who don't have all the tools, or maybe they don't have any at all. We buy him or her all the tools needed to get started. The company owns the tools for the first ninety days, and then after that, the apprentices can use their tool account money to buy the tools from us.

Professional appearance is important for our people. I looked at our uniforms several years ago and thought they looked hot and uncomfortable. "I wouldn't wear that," I thought, "so why am I mandating our employees to wear it?" I put a few options together for new uniforms and asked the technicians which ones they liked. I let them pick because they're the ones who have to wear it every day, and they should be comfortable and look professional when they roll up to a customer's home.

Another program in this area is our gym membership program that reimburses employees for a gym membership. There's an app that employees use to check in when they get to the gym, and then they submit their invoice for the gym membership fee reimbursement through the app. At the end of every month, we get a report from the app that tells us how many times an employee went to the gym, and we get the invoice. Employees receive the fee reimbursement in their paychecks the next week. Personally, I think healthy living is also part of professionalism and professional appearance. We encourage it because if employees are working out and are healthy, they're going to perform better for the customer but also be at their best for themselves, their families, and the company. Beyond starting to exercise through the gym program, a number of our people have quit smoking or achieved their weight loss goals over the last couple of years.

These might seem like small details, but they're critical to professionalism and can't be overlooked. If you overlook small details such as these in your business, your whole service offering falls apart for the customer. It's important to pay attention to the very fine details that help provide a high level of service for both the employees and your customers.

Internal Coaching

Providing service with significance comes down to a lot of coaching internally to help our great people continue to the next level. We've found success with our one-on-one coaching program for technicians and with management. Along with weekly department meetings, managers have one-on-one meetings with every employee in their department. These sessions aren't so much about job duties but more about life in general and building good relationships. Managers discuss how the employee is doing in general, their family, what they're going to do on the weekend, and so on. We've found that creating a good relationship is extremely important because people start to open up, which builds a level of trust. For example, if the manager recommends that the employee try something different in the field to be more successful, the employee trusts that the manager is making that recommendation not because the company is looking out for itself, but rather because we are looking out for the employee and want to see them do better (and ultimately do better for the customer).

The hardest part about such personal, one-on-one sessions is scheduling them. Managers have many people in their departments, and carving out time to sit down weekly with each one individually can sometimes be difficult and can even feel overwhelming.

But in our experience, the level of trust that's built from the fifteen or twenty minutes the manager spends truly taking an interest in what's going on with the employee is difficult to break. We've seen more performance improvements after a one-on-one meeting when job duties weren't even discussed in that meeting. But the employee understands that the company and the manager care about them and want them to perform well and be successful. The manager and employee have an honest conversation over a coffee or tea, and the manager doesn't yell at them for bad performance or even talk about the job duties.

The DiSC profile I discussed in the recruitment section helps managers to communicate effectively in these personal meetings with all kinds of people on their team. Our goal is for both parties to come to the session and express how they feel. For that to happen, the manager needs to communicate with the employee in the employee's style, which they learn from the DiSC profile. It's been very impactful in combination with these one-on-one meetings. I believe it gets to what we're trying to build here, which isn't just a huge moneymaking machine with the technicians as pawns in a big game who produce and never complain. We're trying to change lives. It's very powerful when the root of what you're doing inside your company is a reflection of what you're trying to do outside your company for your customers. Everyone is looking out for each other and knows they can trust everybody on the team.

Building Relationships with Customers

Peterman strives to build lasting relationships with customers. We don't want our customers to be one-time sales, because it means they bought our services out of need and not out of trust. We want each customer's buying decision to be out of trust—trust in our opinions, our knowledge, and our professionalism. We don't try to get as much money out of a customer as we can or measure our technicians' success by how much they sell. We'd probably lose many good technicians if we did, and it would mean we're probably selling things to our customers that they don't really need. If that happens, the customer isn't winning, and we must create a win for the customer. If we don't listen to our customers and empower them through education and our skills and ability, we're never going to get to a win for them because we're never going to uncover their true problem. Peterman's philosophy is to go out there, build a relationship, provide some value for that customer, and always provide service with significance. If we provide the value and significance, the revenue follows because people trust us and will always want to buy from us.

It's important to stay in touch with customers to maintain the relationship and to solicit their opinions. Several times a year, I'll send an email to our entire customer base about an idea for an offering, for example, or some other topic on which I'd like to hear their opinions. I make it easy for customers to respond: "Are you interested in this potential service we're thinking about offering? Click yes or no." It's easy to get a good, representative opinion in this way. I once asked our entire Peterman Protection Club membership to suggest new benefits we could add to the club. I got hundreds of responses that helped us tailor our membership offerings to meet what our customers want most.

We also publish an eight-page color newsletter that we send out to customers each month to educate customers and help them to know us better. Typical contents include employee profiles, a column my dad writes called Fatherly Advice (usually about customer service lessons he's learned), and a column my wife writes directed to women. More than anything, we help our customers see that we're not a faceless company but rather people just like them who enjoy taking care of other people and have a great time doing it too.

Building a sustainable company that grows relies on strong, healthy relationships both inside and outside the organization. Your service will always have significance when you listen to your customers and prove it by giving them the great service they need and expect.

Chapter 8:

Give Customers the Wow Experience

Inquired with Peterman about upgrading and replacing my old, standard water heater with a tankless unit. During the consult, it was pointed out and advised that my money would be better spent on replacing the mess of cast iron drains I had going in my 1950s home before spending money on an upgrade. Very honest conversation and the furthest from a sales pitch as the conversation could have gone. Along the line of "do the need, not the want."

I ended up doing both, along with some PEX additions and couldn't be any happier with the result. From the planning, to the communication, to dealing with a few last-minute additions I wanted to have them complete … Peterman nailed it. Friendly, professional, and knowledgeable every step of the way.

—Matt L.

Think about how you perceive services in your everyday life, whether you hired a plumber, a lawn service, or a heating contractor. We've all experienced satisfactory services, but we don't usually call a friend or post something on Facebook about a satisfactory service. We tell people about an extraordinary experience, one that was so unique we didn't expect it, or it went over and above what we felt was necessary.

I call that a "wow experience" because it can literally make a customer say, "Wow!"

How can companies give customers wow experiences? First, you have to understand that you provide an experience and not a simple service. At Peterman, we don't run service calls. We give customers the wow experience because we want to build lasting relationships, not just one-time transactions. In our industry, people think we provide furnace tune-ups or install water heaters, but we really provide an experience that customers will remember—whether it's positive or negative. The experience starts the second your customer calls you and continues for as long as you maintain a relationship with that customer. The experience consists of all of your interactions with the customer—by mail, email, phone, or in person, whether it's a service call, a follow-up visit, or a regular maintenance check. And customers will remember all of it.

> You should strive to create an experience that's both the best in your industry and the best for any type of service.

What exactly is a wow experience? It's your relationship with your customer and a service experience that's so special, they don't want to do business with any other company. The relationship is a string of interactions that occurs not in an hour but over a lifetime. The experience starts the second your customer calls you and continues for as long as you maintain the relationship. I have the most fun in my job when I'm figuring out creative ways to provide wow experiences, ways that are different and memorable while giving customers the products and services they need and want.

We don't want our customers to remember a negative experience, and you shouldn't either. You should strive to create an experience that's both the best in your industry and the best for any type of service. If you want to give your customers the wow experience, the mentality and commitment to do so has to start with leadership because leaders need to instill it in everyone else. I believe that it starts with treating employees right (giving them the wow experience too) so they'll take care of the customers. I've said many times that Peterman's number-one customer is our employees, and if we don't give them a wow experience, how can we expect them to give our customers a wow experience? The great thing about entrepreneurship is that you, the entrepreneur, are in control. You can build your company any way you want to build it. But if you give your employees a bad experience, probably the only way they'll give your customers a satisfactory experience is out of fear that they'll lose their jobs if they don't. They must understand that the company cares about them so that they care about the customer and are there to help them.

Leaders aren't exempt from participating in the wow experience for the customer. The foundation for it is your actions and your company culture, and your customers feel it every time you're in their homes, send them an email, or talk with them on the phone. Your culture helps create that experience.

I've found in our experience that you should do several important things to create wow experiences consistently.

For the customer:
- Make sure all employees understand their roles in creating the experience.
- Communicate with the customer.
- Be consistent with your service.
- For your company:
- Embrace a growth mindset.
- Network to find ideas for great service inside and outside of your industry.
- Show your company's human side.
- Refuse to be a commodity.

I'll discuss each of these items to help you see how you can create wow experiences for your customers.

Understanding Roles

We're all linked together to provide wow experiences. Over the course of a ten-year relationship with the customer, as many as fifty different people could touch that customer. If we ever find breakdowns in our customer service, it often occurs because one person didn't realize what another person was doing regarding the customer or didn't realize the importance of their particular role in setting expectations. It's a break in the chain. But if we shoot high and try to provide that wow experience instead of just hoping customers are satisfied, there's going to be a lot more leeway for forgiveness when a break in the chain occurs. If I provide an over-the-top experience for the customer each and every time, then any time we do come up short, we'll rebound from that, and we'll keep fighting ahead.

When my dad first started the company, he was alone—the only link in the chain. All customer service started and ended with him, and that's easy to control. As companies grow, however, leaders often forget that the level of communication has to increase simply because if it doesn't, then you often have departments and functions that are siloed, and you get in trouble with customers if one piece doesn't talk to the other. When you have more people, everyone must know their role and understand how others' roles fit in the process.

We teach all employees how they contribute to the experience, along with the importance of consistent communications. For example, let's step through part of a standard service call at Peterman and see how people's roles rely on others in the process.

- Training: The process starts with the training our people receive. We educate our call center employees on heating and cooling systems and everything else we do to give them a working knowledge of the types of problems a customer might have and know what type of technician to send on the call.

- Initial phone call: The call probably resulted from a marketing effort. People might have seen our ads, but possibly they called because friends or family recommended us.

- Marketing message: Our marketing department and our call center must understand our message to customers so we can attract customers who will like our service and handle their calls properly.

- Call center response: Our call center people need to be sympathetic to customers' situations to show them that we understand and are ready to help. Being sympathetic shows them that we understand and are ready to help, and it sets the stage for what the customer is about to experience with our service. This is highly important because it's part of retraining customers to expect higher-quality service. The call center schedules the service call.

- Retrain customers: We set expectations to retrain our customers to expect a wow experience versus a satisfactory experience. We explain what's going to happen on the call and that our service will be different from what they've received in the past. Customers often say, "No one's ever done this before." We tell them it's how we think service is done best.

- Dispatcher: The customer will likely talk with a dispatcher on the day of service who will again set the scene for what will happen on the day of service, providing the technician's name and emailing the customer the technician's photo. The customer already expects this because the call center outlined the process.

- Technician: The technician explains the process again when he or she arrives at the customer's home. The technician must know what the call center told the customer, and he or she learns this from software we have that lets the technician listen to a recording of the phone call. This is an example of how we use different tools and strategies to link our employees' interactions.

It's easy to see how one person's role relies on another's role. Customers are often used to talking with several people at a company and concluding that none of them seems to know what the other is doing.

Internally, we use strategy meetings to examine how we can provide better service, looking objectively at any area or process that we might improve, which also reinforces how people's roles interact. These meetings have paid really big dividends for us. We look objectively at any area or process that we might improve, even if it's just a small improvement. If we're discussing a process, for example, we invite every person involved in that process to discuss it because customers sometimes tell one person something that could improve our process, but we might not know about it if we don't involve everyone in the discussion.

We might discover that people aren't performing their roles, and that's where the whole process falls apart. We set out to look at one process or issue and might find one or more smaller things we can improve. Sometimes we look to improve on something that's already great. For example, our close rate on a particular type of lead was 65 percent, which was over and above our goal for that lead. But we still tried to figure out how we could improve that number and serve the customer better on those particular leads. We've seen great results from having these meetings because we get everyone's perspectives and opinions. Good internal communication like this ensures that all employees are on the same page and performing their roles, which can be the best comfort you can give a customer. The result is a smooth, consistent experience that makes customers happy with your service.

Communicate with the Customer

Speaking to customers person to person on a human level is an integral part of the wow experience. In the process example, you can see how we overcommunicate when explaining what customers will experience with our service. I honestly don't think you can overcommunicate. Companies in our industry often fail because they don't communicate enough.

Communication should be an ongoing effort, not just when you're providing service. We've built a community with our customers through our marketing and advertising efforts, which strive to make people connections. Our customers call our company to help them, but a person arrives at their home, and we want them to know that person. Texting the customer our technician's biography and photo before the service call is one way of doing this. We also publish employee profile articles in our newsletter to help customers know Greg the plumber or John the heating technician. Other newsletter sections list employee anniversaries and birthdays, give customers recipes, and run a coloring contest for kids. My brother and I record all of our own radio commercials, and almost all of our print ads include a photo of us. Customers know who we are and that we're people just like them.

Another good way to communicate is through feedback and responses. We always ask customers for feedback and make it easy for them to provide reviews, but it's important to respond to all feedback. Our technicians always ask the customer, "Was this a five-star experience today?" If the answer is yes, they ask for a review. If the answer is no, they ask, "How can we fix that before I leave today?" Always make sure your customers know that you appreciate them taking time to write reviews that you can to learn how to improve your service. When you provide a wow experience, you empower your customers to recommend your company because they want their family and friends to have wow experiences too. It makes them feel good. If you give your customers something to talk about, they probably will.

We're also extending our training to customers as a way to bring them together with our people and to share knowledge, tips, and experiences. Other companies in our industry might offer seminars to customers, but we're taking it further. For example, I could have a seminar on ten ways to help increase the efficiency of

> All of your communication should be about people and making connections.

your air conditioner, but I'm probably not going to get a lot of people to show up. Much like I want this book to accomplish, my hope is to use our trainings as ways to influence customers to improve their lives and have a real impact on them, so customers are invited to seminars on self-help and personal improvement topics, such as leadership and goal setting. These topics are more relevant to the average person outside of a business context, and customers might even have kids who could benefit. It's using our training inside the company to help those outside the company, and anybody can probably benefit from the message. My hope is that customers will take advantage of this offering and learn more about Peterman and our people in the process.

All of your communication should be about people and making connections. Our customers know whom they're talking with when they call us, and we know them, both of which make it easier to provide the wow experience.

Be Consistent with Your Service

Peterman's rigorous processes aim at providing consistent experiences. We have checklists for every type of service and maintenance we perform. It might seem mundane and methodical, but it keeps everything consistent, and that's what customers want. Can your company deliver a high level of service and replicate it time after time? We use detailed process checklists to stay consistent, but we also leave the technician some leeway to add a personal touch to the experience. Another strategy is doing a video walk-through of a project. When our installation crew goes to the home, they've already watched a video walk-through and know what's expected and what others in the process told the customer.

Even with checklists and other tools for consistency, sometimes things will go wrong that aren't your fault and are out of your control. Because of this, it's important to control the things that you can control, and you should always consider which things you can control in your service offering that will provide a consistent experience. Still, the things you can't control probably won't cause you to lose a customer if you've created a good relationship. Just own up to the mistake and fix it because it's another opportunity to provide the wow experience. The key is to always aim high. If you fall back, you fall back to a pretty good level of service at least. Providing the wow experience consistently gives you a lot more room for error, and your customers will be more forgiving of your mistakes.

Embrace a Growth Mindset

You create the wow experience by always striving to create it and making sure that the company is always growing. People often think that growth means more people, more headaches, and more issues. We look at growth as being able to affect more people positively. Because we provide great service and continually work to make it the best, we feel it's our obligation to give that wow experience to as many people as we can.

Growing doesn't always mean making a company bigger but rather becoming better at what you do and creating a culture of wanting to improve. As you improve your service, your customers will tell others, and growth will happen naturally. A culture of people who are high achievers and who want to improve fuels a company's growth in size, and I think some people are confused about what that means. They want to grow a company by just adding more people and doing more business. But the culture, attitudes, values, and customer philosophy has to grow too. Because Peterman continues to improve, the company becomes larger because people want to join companies that improve and can continually provide more opportunities for people.

Network for Ideas

We get many ideas for creating great experiences from networking with other businesses. Our company belongs to several marketing and trade organizations both inside and outside our industry. I've learned so much from these networks—probably more from networks that aren't industry specific. For example, we use text messaging to confirm service appointments, an idea I took from dentists, who were the first people I saw using texts in that way. Our newsletter is another example. The format was inspired by a newsletter published by a marketing and customer service organization. It really resonated with us as a way to show the human side of Peterman.

You have to be open to new ideas on communicating with customers and providing unique experiences. It's easy to become boxed in by a mindset that says you can't do certain things because they're not the norm in your industry. If you want to provide different experiences, get out of the box, and do things that aren't the norm. When I see good ideas from outside our industry, I figure out how to replicate them. I think it's fun to find an experience that your dentist or grocery store or a restaurant provides and mold it into something that works for you. From the customer's viewpoint, you have something that no one else has, and your experience—your wow experience—is like no other in your industry.

Show Your Company's Human Side

I think showing a company's human side is the biggest part of the wow experience because so few companies do that. Our customers know Peterman is my dad and our family, and employees who have names and are people just like them. We give our customers a personal touch in everything we do, and it's always the little things we do that count.

I've found great ideas for personal touches from outside our industry, particularly from Zappos, which has always done innovative customer service. For example, when their call center people notice that it's someone's birthday or anniversary, they send them flowers. Our call center has a goal each week to send out a specific number of personal notes to customers. It encourages them to have human conversations and make our service personal. For example, if a customer cancels an appointment because a spouse was ill or their pet passed away, we send a personal note that says simply, "We're thinking about you. We know you're going through a tough time." We let the customer know that they can call us whenever they need us. They already know that we want to help them, and the help they need at that moment might be a little support.

Refuse to Be a Commodity

Customers don't have to call us (or any company, for that matter) to get their job done because they have many options. They can buy a water heater from a big box store that will also install it. They could probably get a neighbor to install a furnace. They can even look up DIY instructions for most any home repair issue on YouTube. When your company provides something that customers can get anywhere, it's a commodity. But if you provide the wow experience, it's something more, something customers can't get anywhere else. Committing to giving customers that wow experience every time ensures your company won't be a commodity. Ask yourself what makes your company and your service unique. What makes you special? It's why your experience is a wow experience compared with everything else and why your customers won't have a reason to go elsewhere.

We often joke around here that we wish each service call just said, "Go help this customer" with an address and a name. Often, companies aren't out there to help somebody but rather to sell something or repair something. Customers can feel it when you really want to help them, and it's the essence of the wow experience when they know you care about their happiness and protecting their home. They'll talk about when they genuinely know that the company and its people—everybody they encountered that day, whether in person or on the phone—really cares about them and their home, and taking care of their problem.

Conclusion:

Why We're Different

I read through the introduction to this book again, and it occurred to me while reading it that I have two purposes for writing this book: one is to share the ideas and strategies that have made Peterman Heating, Cooling & Plumbing a success, and the other is to honor my dad, Pete Peterman, and what he started and what we continue to build. I was just a little kid when Dad started his business in our garage. Thinking back on my childhood and my memories of Dad at that time, I didn't really know much about what he was doing. I knew it had something to do with heating and air conditioning, but I clearly remember how committed he was to his work. There were very few mornings when I woke up and he wasn't already gone to work helping customers, getting his guys out doing calls, or working on his tasks to keep the company running. I also remember many times when he came home late at night, especially when the weather was extremely hot or cold because that's when his customers needed him the most. My mom tells stories about how Dad would often be out working at all hours of the night, making sure that he took care of the people he was committed to help.

When I first started working in the business, I played a game trying to beat Dad to work. Could I arrive there before he did? Sometimes I did, and sometimes I didn't. Dad's still the best at what he does. But that little game was my way of showing him my own commitment to hard work and to making Peterman Heating, Cooling & Plumbing successful. My brother, Tyler, and I learned that kind of commitment from Dad—and a lot more. He taught us that although we might not always know the answers to the problems we encounter, one thing we can control is how hard we work, how much effort we put into what we do. He also taught us that if we're doing the right thing, good things will happen, and we'll find the answers to the problems. That's the thing I love most about Dad: his hard work and his values and morals—he never lost sight of any of that while growing the business. Hard work is often associated with long hours, and people who work long hours are often called workaholics. But Dad didn't work hard for work's sake, and overall he didn't do it for the money. He always made time for his family and still managed to grow an extremely successful business. I vividly remember my mother saying that no matter how busy he was, he never missed any of my or my brother's football, basketball, or baseball games. Sometimes he'd even coach a baseball game and then put his work clothes back on and go back to work.

> That's the thing I love most about Dad: his hard work and his values and morals—he never lost sight of any of that while growing the business.

Dad started the business and ran it by himself for a while, but the ultimate customer he tried to serve at the time was his family. Then the business grew and evolved to serve employees and customers, but I think the stories about him not missing our games and still managing to grow such a successful business point to the fact that you can work as hard as you want, and you can build a huge business, but it won't be worth it in the end if you don't do it for the right reasons.

I think that although this held true when the company was very small and the only people whom Dad was serving were my brother, my mom, and me to make sure that we had what we needed and never went without, that still holds true today. We work very, very hard, and our people work very, very hard. But what makes all that hard work worth it is the fact that we've all created a place where we can grow, become better people, and become better for our customers and our families. The hard work is worth it when we have those values aligned correctly, but you can go off course when you don't have those values aligned—for example, when you're working to simply make money versus working for a greater purpose, such as setting an example for your son or daughter. That's when you're growing as a person. Peterman has continued to evolve from a business that merely serves employees to a vehicle that affect's people's lives in positive ways, and the special culture we've created has become the foundation of our growth and success. At that point, people came to work for us who also understood that and wanted to serve the company—not work at Peterman, not clock in and out, but serve the company. When the team members and the owners are both on the same page with aligned values like that, the customer is served every single time with extraordinary service.

Our ultimate mission is to be a kind of beacon for people who hold these beliefs, who want to do things differently and better, and who aren't satisfied with the status quo of the trades or what a contractor should be for a customer. We feel that there's a better way, and we want to change our industry. We want every service call and every installation to reflect the fact that there's a deeper purpose behind what we do. It's not about money, it's not about the next job, and it's not selling more things to the customers. It's about making the world a better place and hopefully affecting those who will come after us.

Someone once asked me to list my best advice on how to grow a business. They wanted to know what process and procedures we use to run the business smoothly every day. But when I thought about a list of advice, it didn't include processes and procedures. I believe that you have to get your priorities and focus straight first, and then things like processes and procedures will work themselves out. I've found that if you focus on the following, you can't stop the growth, and your business will be different from all the others in your industry:

- Align your business with what's truly important to you, and understand that your company has to serve more than just you, the owner. Serve everyone who's involved in the business—they'll serve the company and take care of the customers.
- Focus on your people. Find the best, commit to their growth, and make it your mission to create the best work culture that you can, built on your core values.
- Hire the right people, and empower them to succeed. Give them a platform to be successful, and they'll never stop wanting to improve themselves and the company.
- Instill hope, care, and compassion in the lives of your employees, and they'll start dreaming, setting goals, and accomplishing great things.
- Don't hold anyone back. Make your company a place where employees have no limits.
- Truly care about each person and treat everyone fairly, no matter who they are—employees, customers, and especially yourself.

- Set an example for everyone, including employees and customers, but especially your own sons and daughters, who are the next generation that will affect the world.
- Strive to find the better way and make an impact on your industry. Let everything you do in your business reflect the deeper purpose behind what you do.
- Remember that what you do is about making the world a better place and hopefully affecting those who come after you. It really isn't about the money, the next job, or selling more products.

One wall in the front lobby of our building is covered with quotes about what makes Peterman Heating, Cooling & Plumbing different from other companies. We call it our culture wall. The quotes on it are from our employees who, in their ninety-day reviews, write down what employees and customers say makes us different and the things we do that make us different. The culture wall is truly a testimony to our success and shows why we couldn't stop the growth at Peterman. It also honors Dad and the company he started. I could probably write another book about how to grow a successful company just from all of those quotes. Seeing that wall every day makes me proud, but more important, it makes everyone who works at Peterman proud to work for us, and they know they're a major part of our success.

I hope this book will help business owners use what we've learned to improve their companies. I've described how Peterman went from a one-man operation in a garage to the successful company we are today that employs more than 120 people and affects the lives of many, many more. Anyone who wants to learn even more can watch our videos on YouTube or listen to our podcasts, both of which include our actual leadership series seminars. I also hope the book encourages more customers to expect more from the companies with which they do business. Ultimately, we want to lift each other up—companies lift customers in their times of need with the products and services they provide, and customers lift companies by holding them to higher standards and rewarding great service with reviews and recommendations.

I wish you much success and that you, too, can't stop the growth and will make the greatest impact you can on your people, your industry, and the world.

Contact

Email: chad@petermanhvac.com
LinkedIn: linkedin.com/in/chad-m-peterman
www.petermanhvac.com
LinkedIn: https://www.linkedin.com/company/petermanhvac/
Facebook: @PetermanHVAC
Podcast: https://podcasts.apple.com/au/podcast/
cant-stop-the-growth/id1453293843

9 781642 251586